CW00860280

Life, Liberty, and Injustice

EDUCATION, BULLYING, AND HATE CRIMES

Khadijah Tiya Muhammad

PAGE PUBLISHING, INC.
Conneaut Lake, PA

First originally published by Page Publishing 2019

ISBN 978-1-64424-382-4 (pbk)
ISBN 978-1-64424-385-5 (hc)
ISBN 978-1-64424-384-8 (digital)

Printed in the United States of America

This book is dedicated to my Mother, Father,
Bessie (2nd mother), sisters, brother, daughter Alysha,
Alex Matthews (cover designer), all my wonderful family
members and friends, Courtney Mathews, Deborah
Colvin, Ralph Smith, Sharon Wheeling, Samuel
Abduel Majied and my West Virginia family.

Contents

Abstract 6

Chapter 1: Mental Health Myths and Facts 42

Chapter 2: American Psychological Association 46

Chapter 3: Bullying and Cyberbullying 49

Chapter 4: American Humane Association 51

Chapter 5: Psychological Issues Are Common Effects of
Bullying 58

Chapter 6: Some Definitions for different forms of
BULLYING 65

Chapter 7: International Journal of
NEUROPSYCHOTHERAPY (IJNPT) 74

Chapter 8: Know Your Right Street Harassment 77

Chapter 9: 76+ COUNTRIES WHERE
HOMOSEXUALITY IS ILLEGAL 101

Chapter 10: The **FBI** Federal Bureau of Investigation 109

Abstract

When the educational system and daily life fail a mother and her bi-racial male teenager in exercising his rights to an education and a safe environment, the fight costs him, his dreams of a better life and how things change around them. And the courage of one woman to see his pain and understand the harassment on his life, and what they had to go through to make the school system and others aware of the liberties and injustice both (teenager and woman) were facing behind closed doors, was unbelievable through the end, for justice. Also, what they had in common in the end would be more than saving others, than saving themselves. "If only the nation would have listened, still." Bullying is a universal problem, in the workplace, communities, our household, schools and more. Will you know a bully when you see, hear or understand the actions, as a crime?

T his is a story about *life, liberty and injustice* concerning all of us, also the way we live and think about the times we are living in, mainly the direction of what our children and our communities will become and what we are facing in the near future. *We have the right to an education, as well as the right to enjoy a safe environment in our schools, churches, communities and workplaces.*

I must remind you that while reading, you must have an open mind about your life and the lives of other people around you, maybe at work, at home, in an educational environment or in your daily life. Step out of your comfort zone and take a walk on this side of life, where many people have chosen to forget and some will never even experienced, still remember. But secretly, in the closets of life, in a world of so many liberties for everybody today, you may have had some experiences of your own form of this word, in this world, known as injustice. No matter what country you are from, there are a minority of people that are able to express to you, the feeling of what life is like in a world of liberties, that you are not entitled to enjoy because of the injustice bestowed on you, during or at this time and place where people just don't care how people are living.

My reason for writing this book was to inform the media, the public, and those individuals at the time, how unconcerned we are for one another, like a silent lynching of the mind and soul. We have been falling so long into a world of unconsciousness. We may not know we are there yet because of our lifestyles of being too busy, living for the Joneses, reflecting that everything must look good all the time so we may get ahead, without concern for our fellow man, woman or child. How low do we go before we make a turn toward awareness of the human soul, or are we, you or I, at a point of no return to find peace within this world, on this planet, or in this nation? We are asked to pledge allegiance to our flag at the beginning of every sporting event or gathering, reminding some of us, when shall we overcome one day? When will we stop seeing or hearing from the graves of our darkest hours?

This story starts off in many settings. You may find a part of your life along the way of good memories or some bad moments of the past. However, this story is in Charleston, West Virginia, amid size city and a state full of warmth in landscaping and family traditions, known to be called *Wild, Wonderful state of West Virginia*. It is a home to many wildlife (animals) and hardworking families, where agriculture, coal mining, and chemical plant industries are the source of most of the family income. It is a state often admired for it's beautiful mountains, trees, flooding rivers, and bridges, and this place has been blessed with a natural resource for hunting as well as a lot of land, with rich quality of life. It is a place where people are still sits on the porch or in the yard sharing a story or two of something in the past, present or future, especially that high school or college game, they love.

This is an ideal place to raise a family, leaving behind the riff raff and the fast pace of urban lifestyle. To some, this is a huge change after just leaving Los Angeles, California, but migrating to this place is considered a fresh start. However, it is to others, like coming back home to the basics of life. Often, we hear the cliché "There's no place like home." While that's true, in essence it's also untrue because of environmental changes like family dynamics, economy, and lifestyle choices.

In the state of Michigan, the city Detroit, name from the French, "will rise from the ashes" is on a statue outside the City Hall. Detroit is also known to be a blue-collar town and its riches. Called the Motor City, known all over the world for the music of Motown Records and surrounded by a world class automotive industry with General Motors (GM), Ford Automobiles, and Chrysler Motors for a middle class living. Many families move from the south, east, west, and overseas for work and to start businesses in the industrial communities. This is a place where hard work is considered normal, and it has a great history to tell. Generations of families have migrated to this place in order to have a chance at the American dream. Some have even gone as far as to drop out of school for an opportunity to make big money on the assembly line, making a better life for their families to grow in the middle- class lifestyle.

Moving to West Virginia was great for me, with the fresh air, mountains, trees and flood of rivers through the cities. Here I am surrounded by the beautiful hills a peaceful bliss filled with tranquility, for a lady like me imagined it to be the beginning of something I would never forget. There are moments in your life you have a spiritual awakening of who and what you are to do. And for me, this was one of them. A vision came to me by the divine when I was just a little girl, and although it hadn't materialized at that moment, it sure became a reality when I met Bobby Smith and his mother, Sharon. I thought most of all, how wonderful it is having a beautiful daughter and family, a child that is able to grow from a baby into an adult that enjoys the basics of life by running around the neighborhoods full of family and friends of different religions and biracial ethic (black and white), backgrounds, dancing, swimming, being a Brownies (Girl Scouts), and so on. Not knowing the dangers of the world, at times we enjoy looking out the kitchen or living room window to see there is a deer or two in the yard. We enjoy gardening fresh vegetables on individual properties, seeing horses behind fences running on the acres of the neighbors' lands and much more. Sometimes it looks like a Norman Rockwell picture in a rural area.

Bobby A. Smith, a bi-racial young man (black/white) was 15 fifteen years old when his mother Sharon Smith (white), decided to move back to her home state West Virginia, in 1992, Ms. Smith moved from Detroit's Inter City to Poca, West Virginia, (Putnam County), one small town out of many where Bobby lived and attended Madison High School, a very nice and clean looking school, a lot of school clubs and great sport activities. Most students were bused in on the yellow school buses and have grown up together, but for Bobby this was a very big change from the Motor City school system.

In 1993, many things in life were changing so rapidly people didn't quite understand or thought about what was going on, enough to question. Some would say, "It looks like we are going back in time," while others grab hold of their different faiths to embrace hope in order to make life preparations for a future truly unknown.

There were political changes accusing foreign policy changes, and jobs were in the beginning stages of being shipped overseas. The cost of living hit home for many shaken up by job losses and their day to day security became unsure. People began to have various lifestyle changes; deciding whether to come out of the closet or to just stay in and lead a quiet life. Communities became a challenge because of the economy; homeowners were faced with more renters moving in the neighborhoods which caused some areas to change as well, not always for the better. Many thought we were losing our United States of America, in the way most people have known it to be, a healthy nation in the land of plenty with the rights of a good life, with food, clothes, shelter, transportation, education, a job and even more.

View of the city of Detroit, Michigan, named by the French, word for "strait" and the French called the Detroit River "le Detroit du Lac Eric, meaning "the strait of Lake Eric"

June 23, 1963 in Detroit, Michigan, USA
Martin Luther King's "Freedom March"

State of West Virginia, City of Charleston

West Virginia Coal Train and coal miner at working

The different states like those of Michigan and West Virginia, took on a whole new parental concern, certainly for the safety of the kids, especially when walking to and from school each day. The constant problems of kids fighting over designer clothing causing the loss of lives, became a major problem in the metropolitan area. In the rural area, this was not even considered a problem. Metropolitan living was being challenged, even your safety in your own home. The neighborhoods by far were changing unbelievably. As man became more aware of what was going on in the Detroit management system, less police were governing the streets because of less money given to the city as well as to the police department. Many families decided to move toward the suburban areas for a safe learning environment for their kids, as well as for a simpler lifestyle. These crimes were different; they depended on what a kid wore to school. Individuals started carrying guns for protection from crimes. Guns were so plentiful in the community where children lived. Drugs and drug use, domestic violence, and robbery which caused many unstable home environments, these were big concerns for everyone, especially single parents and hardworking parents with children going to and from school.

Mayor Coleman A. Young and the communities, City of Detroit

The city of Detroit, under the late Honorable Coleman A. Young, things were moving forward for African Americans. Opportunities were now available for them to grow in the communities and jobs were offered to exercise their ability to have an exciting city, like during the Motown days. The local citizens were living good healthy lifestyles, so they were able to buy nice houses, and cars, and send their kids to good schools and colleges to receive great educations. Many could see a bright future in politics or working in the political arena and in other cities jobs were available. During that time many moved from the south for better jobs in the automobile industry.

But time had changed in many ways, in regard to opportunities; some people sold other people out for jobs and wealth, not recognizing some things were in place for the future of the kids and the communities. It seemed like a slow death for all. There wasn't a plan for any of the mistakes made in governing our lives, just as the days of integration and freeing of the slaves. The school systems were not given the best leadership roles needed or the overseers were not handling things in the right order for the kids and communities. The City of Detroit, Police Department was being challenged by management and communities funding to run the precincts, causing some to close their doors, which opened the door for the negative thinker, the criminals.

Now this is what Ms. Smith had face concerning her son. She had a love for Detroit however, she decided to move back to Putnam County, in West Virginia. She was hoping for a safe learning environment that would provide a quality education for her again for Bobby as well as her family's support for her son. Even I, understood how hard it is to rear children alone and how demanding it can be, so for that reason I decided to relocate to West Virginia in order to be with my partner and raise our daughter together. After living there for some time, I felt compelled to do something good for my community. A productive environment provides a healthy foundation, it gives one a sense of peace and safety within, when you are in a state understanding and growth. Volunteering provided that for me. It caused me to step out of my comfort zone. By doing so, I saw many opportunities where a difference could be made, where change could take place. I worked together with others to grow and exercise my skills constructively, after being there a while.

The Civil Right era, even as a free man and Slavery is the ownership of one human being by another.

This is about a woman deciding to campaign for the presidency of the Charleston Chapter of the NAACP, the National Association for the Advancement of Colored People, an organization that fought for human rights for minorities, since 1909, and changed many unjust acts of the civil rights in the United States of America. For over four hundred years, oppression and fear of bullying to maintain injustice has been placed on some human beings man, woman or children in U.S.A. and in other countries. After campaigning, on February 26, 1993, I became the new president of the NAACP Charleston Chapter. This was my calling one day in my life's journey, to help all mankind through public service. What I said, being a Muslim in a Christian organization was not easy. Just like being a person of color (different race) wasn't easy in this world in the USA, being a woman working wasn't easy in a man's world, but I loved it. It was a hard stone to walk on at first unto people begin to become more open minded, and aware that people are people when they are serious by helping, at a time of need.

The state of West Virginia was in a stage of growth when it came to diversification of culture to become a part of servicing a position in public offices. The NAACP office was located inside the basement of a women's community club. The first time I open the door to the office I saw a lot of work ahead for me. A place that wasn't used in a long time, it was dirty, dusty and dark, in need of a lot of love for the job by spending a lot of time there and being real about bringing the office back to the public, so it would express pride and getting down to business with respect for the organization, based on the civil rights movement of the past along with present goals. The goal must remain, "A right to be considered equal and be treated with respect". My understanding as president was to reach out to the community building trust to believe that the NAACP was back and was serious about being a part of the daily structure and growing our community within the local state system, for the better. First, I needed to know where to start with the communities needs and what this office stood for to be a part of the future as well as to regain a seat at the table for negotiations on economic growth in the area of banking opportunities in loans, jobs or savings government jobs in civil service, positions of power, a job bank for hire and dialogues with other cultures on religion, services, health, and understanding.

Shortly after my victory and after weeks of getting the office together, having some community meetings, as well as recruiting volunteers to help in the offices, and working with local, state movers and shakers, the office was coming together. In the spring of 1993 semester, I was in the office alone with the door open during the evening, moving around, posting jobs and posters on the boards, I hear footsteps coming down the hallway; then I turned around to look at the door. This was when she saw Ms. Sharon Smith standing in the doorway, a medium height, full sized Caucasian woman. She came to the NAACP office door, seeking help for son. Maybe someone else may have wondered. "Why? Or what is a Caucasian woman coming to the NAACP office for?" I understood the word minority does not just mean for blacks only and as I stated before, the world was changing so fast. But to understand the change is to know where we are going in the world as human beings and what does change mean to us as a people? Looking back, I grew up in and around culture in my younger days, I had no doubt where this was going. I said to her, "Hello, welcome to the NAACP office. How may I help you?" I did not find it strange to see this woman in the doorway. She replied, "Well, I was looking for someone to talk with, concerning my son and a problem he is having at his school, I have tried to do everything in my power to seek help for him, I have not received any help or concern for what he is going through." At this point, Ms. Sharon Smith's emotions made it, sure she needed to talk to someone from the NAACP office, so she was asked to have a seat, so more could be understood about what was going on, to see if this was where she should be helped or if this was something of the organization's concern, or maybe refer her to another organization.

As Ms. Smith began talking, she expressed more of her pain and frustration as a mother seeing her son go through this day to day suffering. Slowly tears were flooding from her eyes, as I, the president was taking notes and continued to ask questions, being careful and aware of her pain. Meanwhile, it was clear a follow up was needed on this matter. Each step of the way, it was really that their path and journey would become a future nightmare around the world. It was unbelievable how this matter was being handled by the adults in the school system and the parents' behaviors in dealing with the problem once they were faced with the truth.

At this point, I scheduled a time to meet with Bobby and his mother again, at their home, in a setting that was comfortable for Bobby. This was where we needed him to talk about the problem, with the understanding that I wasn't just another person not really concerned, just doing her job, if you know what that meant like talking to a wall and getting no action of consideration or concern. Many people can relate to this at one point in their lives. If not, keep living long enough. Or keep waiting for an answer and waiting, and now it's too late to be fixed. At the Smith home, I could feel the warmth of a mother doing her best to make a home for her kid. Ms. Smith loved her son deeply. She would do whatever to find justice and protection for him. Remember she decided to move back to West Virginia in 1992, this is where she grew up. She had family here, her mother, sister, and cousins. The Smiths were like some of the average West Virginia family, living within their means, working toward the American dream of having a goal for her son in the comfort of what she remembered growing up around family.

This was the beginning of how this bullying and hate crime problems unfold. Bobby was a handsome young man and mild mannered. He had a nice height for his age, a build like an athlete in basketball or baseball sports, caramel skin, and groomed haircut, and skin. He was neatly dressed and up to date as a ball player in gym shoes. His grades were good. He was not a problem student when this matter came into play, and he was a very talented basketball player on the high school team. His goal was to go to college on a scholarship and get his degree in whatever (we never got to that point of understanding), be able to take care of his mother, get married and have a wonderful family. That was one thing Ms. Smith, wanted for him as well. She explained why she moved back to West Virginia to keep her son safe from the urban life. She was very worried that he would get killed because of the violence going on in the streets, at that time, dealing with the youth in street crimes, and being a single parent. She continued to say, "My son is a good boy. He is not doing well with this kind of problem being from the big city, where words and actions are not taken lightly. Knowing he is not being able to react in a verbal matter, plus a feeling of being alone." Not having the schools understanding in this matter wasn't cool or safe for a young man's self-esteem in a new environment.

The white teenage girls were really drawn to him like most girls are toward athletes, and he was likable, but the problem was that Madison High School was a predominantly white school, with five or less African American students, in high school. Do the math. This may be considered nothing to Bobby, but to another males or adults, this was not the right way to go, knowing it was jealousy. So being bi-racial, Bobby Smith at the age of fifteen years old began to experience firsthand bullying, prejudice, and hatred, known as hate crimes. In the state of West Virginia, some form of outdoor sports was known to be a natural thing to do, like hunting, fishing, bungee jumping, dirt car riding, golf and more. So, for some people this may be another day in the park, not something most people would even concern themselves with for the most part or even worry about, if you know what I mean.

However, it was someone's child going through this, Bobby was terrorized every day, in school, on the school bus and even while he was at the comfort of his own home, after school. Let's say beyond child play, he would be told that as a nigger, he would be killed, as well as they were going coon hunting. He was called names like Half Breed and "Nigger", and many of his white friends were called "wigger" (wannabe nigger). He was being tormented within the confines of his own living environment. In the darkness of night, in the area of the dusty road going pass the home where Bobby lived, the bullies would drive by in an orange pickup truck playing loud confederate music. Until one day his cat was found dead on the property, at their entrance way. Another time a noose was found hanging on a tree near his trailer home. Being harassed and bullied constantly began to take its toll upon Bobby's total being, his state of mind. He was deeply depressed to the point of not wanting to go to school. Sitting home every day robbed him of his dreams, and it was as if they had stolen the golden high school moments of what each kid is entitled to have and want to remember, it was the last semester of school before the summer.

Anger filled his soul because of a failing school system that proved how unwilling and uncaring it was, by not believing that his life or civil liberties were ever challenged, until the higher authorities stepped in.

A week later I went to Madison High School, to talk with Ray Wright, the school principal in order to get to the bottom of this whole ordeal but throughout the dialogue Mr. Wright denied the allegations of a hate crime of this magnitude existing in his school or was apparent to any staff or student on his watch. His approach to this sensitive issue was very casual and of no concern to him. It was as though he himself was a former KKK member, and this was a moment back in time of **Emmett Louis Till**. For those whom are not aware of Emmett's story in August 28, 1955 a fourteen years old boy from Chicago was visiting his aunt, uncle and cousin for the summer in Money, Mississippi. They decided to go to town. At the store Emmett wanted to purchase a stick of gum. Ashamed of his stuttering, he was told to whistle for attention, which he did that moment to get the clerks to help him. The lady clerk misunderstood the boy's issue of stuttering and expressed to her husband what was done at the store by Emmett. A day later, two men showed up at his uncle's home to remove this young man from the house, so they could terrorize Emmett for whistling at his wife in the store. He was missing for four days, found by a man fishing twenty miles from Money, in the Tallahatchie River Hodges, weighed down by a seventy-five-pound cotton gin fan that was on barbed wire. Also, he was brutally beaten badly, before he was shot through the head. His trail was the first great media event of the civil rights movement, in the state of Mississippi.

Roy Bryant and J. W. Milam during their 1955 trial

Emmett Till, fourteen years old

Emmett Till age fourteen years old and his mother Mamie E. Mobley

Another story, in the month of June 1951, Rev. Oliver Brown, a father went before the U.S. District Court system to testify why he wanted his daughter Linda Brown, to go to an all-white school in his neighborhood of Topeka, Kansas; not Monroe Elementary School where all black children had to go which was a mile away. The chil-

dren would wait for the bus to come at 8:00a.m. for the thirty min-
utes ride to school, sometimes waiting for the bus in the cold, snow,
or rain, even when the bus was late. After Mr. Brown decided that all
schools should be equal for all, forcing his daughter to travel a significant distance to elementary school due to segregation, the NAACP
stepped in to appeal the decision by taking the complaint to the high
court in the land. Under the legal counsel of Thurgood Marshall,
Robert Carter and Constance Motley they showed that segregation
can actually damages children that are not treated equal, with images
damaging the self-esteem and personality of the children. This was
the birth of Brown vs. Board of Education case.

At that moment I knew Ms. Smith did have a huge problem
on her hand. Also, her son would not be safe in school based on the
hate crime was waiting in school, nor was he protected by those in
authority at the school. So, I had to make some big decisions on how
to address the member of the NAACP on this matter, without making it go unnoticed by those in the community, for Bobby's safety.

The next step was to take this issue to the school board where
Dr. Tracey McDonald, was the superintendent along with all the
other school board members, Ted McClain, Tim Star, Paul Northern
Jr., Dale M. Tyler and Steve Anderson. First off, the setting was an
average size room, not real small so you are aware of the movement
of the school board and any one in the building attending the school
board meeting. While we waited patiently, and for a long time, as
they did whatever, as we waited for our turn. I explained to them
the hate crime that had taken place within their district at Madison
High. They said, "Let us talk this over." We stood in the hallway,
again waiting patiently while Ms. Smith and I experienced something we would never forget or believe, knowing her son was at home
with a deep pain in his heart and soul trying to understand if this
problem would finally be addressed. The school board member of
six, all there at that time, retreated to a back room and began to
laugh loudly continuously, as if we weren't hearing them clearly. We
couldn't believe that they felt someone being terrorized in school was
a joking matter. I informed them that we would be moving forward
on the case. After going over the investigation of the Bobby Smith

file, members of the NAACP legal department, Mr. Bert Hemp the Council of our chapter, and I decided to handle this case as a serious problem of safety and hatred. Then I notified the FBI, the state government, even the local newspaper, to inform the public of this and that any hate crimes against anyone left alone, with no disregard for any child's safety, while in the school's authority, would not be tolerated.

During a press conference Mrs. Smith stated. "Dr. McDonald showed no remorse or anything. A joke is a joke, but to say you will take a life, is no joke. Mr. Wright, the principal did nothing to stop the harassment which started at the beginning of the school year until April 13, to the time Ms. Smith withdrew her son from the school. Ms. Smith said that the three students who had prominent roles in the harassment had already confessed to some violation of the state law and were juveniles at the time of the incident. Before I met with the school board again, the Putnam County sheriff's deputy and the FBI would be doing their investigation this case.

Once the investigation began, Ms. Lisa Clark, the vice principal, shared with Ms. Smith that she heard a student say something inappropriate to Bobby and that it was brought to the principal's attention, yet he decided that it was nothing to focus on. She expressed her feelings about it all, saying, "I didn't think it was an adequate reaction to what I heard and felt."

The four students that were involved in the Madison High racial case were all on the high school football team, a little overweight, average looking, and all were mama's boys. They didn't like blacks and were bullies. They came from two parent households, living in fine areas. They had been using their entitlement to do whatever, as they were spoiled in getting their way at home, as if they were better than anyone else in the community. We had known that their parents would give them things in return by being a boy and an athlete. Bobby came from a single parent household with a mother trying to make ends meet, living in a trailer park. Her only hope was that her son would earn a scholarship to college, for the betterment of his future.

The FBI investigation report was very serious. They told of the remark they heard, Bobby being called, "nigger" and they were going "coon hunting" for him, also doing more thing we could not believe. What Ms. Smith heard made her sadder for her son, Bobby, and still he did not want to go to school. Bobby had so much anger. Now Ms. Smith understood; she just couldn't believe her son was going through so much because of the color of his skin. Remember his mother was white. To see her son being hurt, that showed her mother's love. She wasn't going to allow this to continue.

The NAACP and Mrs. Smith set up a press conference at the NAACP meeting room. There Mrs. Smith explained to the press that someone killed the family cat by smashing its skull. At the beginning of the year, they threw a pear at him, so they were hunting him down and telling him they were going to hurt him in front of the school staff. Mrs. Smith said, "I wanted my son to be safe. That is why I left Detroit, to be a part of a system that had a lot to offer my child and have a life around my family. I could have stated in the city. I just thank God my son was strong even to handle the harassment, even though it is killing him not to hurt them back for the pain they caused him."

These four students were suspended from school for the harassment inflicted upon Bobby Smith. As a result, no confederate paraphernalia was to be seen on lockers or worn by any students on school grounds. I was contacted by the human rights director Dwayne Stephens, of the governor's office, to produce a report on the Smith's case for the governor and sit down with all parties at the state level to put together the foundation on formulation of a program that would send positive anti bullying messages to the community. The United State Senator Rockefeller's office wrote a letter to me, giving their support for stepping in and standing up on this crime. I remember going to a local merchant in the area who had a great business. He knew me for coming to his business to look at cars. When the case was being investigated, his responses to me were "Are you starting trouble?" It was sad to know that even someone on his level looked at this as not being so serious, that NAACP overreacting to make this a case. But Bobby was forced to become home schooled, for the remaining semester of that school year.

In a closed juvenile hearing three boys were formally charged and found guilty in the State of West Virginia Twenty Ninth Judicial Circuit Court by Judge O.C. Spaulding. All boys cried in court once the judge sentenced them to constitute formal charges for violating the civil rights of Bobby Smith. As they began crying, I'm sure it was out of fear of not knowing what was awaiting them as they were ordered to be taken away for the whole summer to a youth institution for boys for mental evaluations, a far distance from the secured environment with their parents. In that room that day, once they heard they were being taken away from their parents' comforts, tears and fear set in their eyes, fear of being locked up for the summer. Once they were in the institution, for bad boys they weren't the bad bullies anymore, sleeping among other bad boys and eating the food, in an environment the three would not be able to control. I was not sure of their future, but I was sure that they would be doing a lot of thinking about the feelings of others and their right to life, liberties and the injustice they bestowed on Bobby, that were beyond child's play.

Ms. Smith requested a letter of apology from the boys to her son to act as a catalyst for his healing process. The letter was granted and signed by the students encouraging him to attend Madison High without any wall of prejudice. Bobby would be going to another school in another county that is welcoming him in the fall, August 1993. He was also seeing a counseling therapist for phobias he never had before, said Ms. Smith. However, the students at Madison High School got together to sign an apology letter to wish for him to return and show that they did not have any racial feeling for him.

By November 1993, Ms. Smith, Bobby and I were contacted by two of the most popular daytime syndication shows, The Jerry Springer Show and The Phil Donahue Show, to share our story. I felt it wasn't a good thing for us to appear on the Jerry Springer Show, there with the KKK members and talking about racism would not do justice for Bobby Smith. It was nothing to laugh or fight about or argue any points of justice. However, The Phil Donahue Show was the right setting to bring awareness to the nation of what was the silent killer of the future, a very serious crime of hate and bullying among children. I tried to make it very clear that we as a nation, "we are in need, we must be more aware of what our kids are saying and doing to others in their school settings, even on the streets." We have felt our civil liberties, hate crimes, bullying, and the life of a human being needed to be addressed to our nation. The Phil Donohue Show gave us an opening to express her foresight that we are on a very sick cycle, that we were not ready to enter the opportunity to inform the public of this growing wave of crime better known at that time as, hate crimes (bullying).

In the past, the KKK was filtering hate crimes on people of color and religion. Also, Adolf Hitler's blossoming haltered of the Jews became part of the organization's political platform, crimes on the Jews. Now oversees crimes of religion and origins were continuing.

Looking back at how time and civil rights matters have changed, but today some things are in settled terms and are sometimes unbelievable. Race against race, religion against religion, sex against sex and cultural differences are always what we are afraid of most, not understanding change or something else being liked in their environment, which bullies wish to control. Being welcomed and helpful to others in some way is looked at as being easy or weak, but in other countries, it's honorable to be that way in their environment.

If we don't adhere to what our children are saying about one another on the cyber network, bullying with children as if they were a cyber-bullying gang, using all social networks that are available to them, as well as bully texting to hurt one another then a huge number of kids will be lost, one by one. Education is learning cultural awareness along with personal experience, thereby respecting one another in the same space. This is not a matter of where they live or how much is the family's income. Bullying still exists on all levels. There are so many similar society backgrounds today. Now that parents are so busy providing, they aren't aware as they should of their children. Please don't be confused either to understand the real issue, because time will continue to tell us the truth.

Just look back, you will see how civil rights matters have not changed very much. Today things are said and done more subtly yet unbelievably race against race, religion against religion, and sexuality against sexuality, as well as cultural differences. Still look how others think they may be better than the other. When we are afraid of change or of someone else becoming a part of our environment we get on the defensive. Are we too busy to notice or just don't want to be involved in stopping the way others are being harassed in some form or fashion? Until it hits home.

For each bullying incident and hate crime incident, I feel their pain. I look back on two things that stay on my mind. What would have happened to Bobby if his mother never came to the NAACP office? That look in Bobby's eyes, the body language that he was showing was like a person tired and at the point of wanting to fight back. Each time I would talk to him, I would say, "Bobby, stay strong; please don't do anything to hurt your rights to life and liberty to go to school again." Don't do anything crazy. There is an old saying, "You can kick a dog but so many times before the dog will bite back." The NAACP was his last chance and I was his last chance for him to believe someone wanted to help him. He was mad and angry at the system for not protecting him and for turning a cheek. I have often wondered why we as humans never listen to our instinct on what words and how far will playing go, before we considered a crime is in the making, by what is being said and the way students are suffering among one another. As parents and staff of the school systems, we must take a step back to focus on our children. They're raising themselves to take on emotional journeys that are maybe too much to explain to a parent or authority, but our kids need to work together to help each other to know when someone has gone too far. We must become more aware in our homes; sometimes we are more aware of our homes than our kids, when our focus should be on children, family, and the communities, even the ones around us. This is what makes a village a home, by looking out for your neighbor, going back to the basics of caring for children, teaching them to care for one another while enjoying the journey of being kids with structure. Yes, it takes a village (community) to raise a child.

After graduating high school, Bobby opted not to pursue a college degree. He moved back to Detroit, where he became a father working odd jobs here and there. He is back to the street game of life, liberty, and just us. He still plays basketball, only on the street courts. Yes, we worked hard to save this young man. We may have won the war on bullying and school violence in the state of West Virginia, however, Bobby has paid a bigger price in his mind, losing his dreams at the same time, as if he were robbed. Only this time the big city did not rob him, it was the nice place, wherever that was and could be an illusion of what is right in front of us but not wanting to face. Injustice is everywhere. It can catch you on your path to your dreams. As parents we all have dreams and goals for our children, yet when their dreams are taken from them by way of other people, it's like losing a part of you too.

Please understand something first. To lose your way is more than just regrouping as an adult, but to lose yourself as a kid or an adult depending on each person, the school system should care for your safety and your future, because it is your rights, even a law or the rules in whatever matters. If not, you will become "lost," not for a minute, some for life. In this case, the time invested in Bobby's goal was lost by some adults of authority as well, to be or not to be in good control of his or her job. Now the word lost (adjective) means (1) Unable to find one's way. (2.a) No longer in one's possession. (2.b) No longer practiced or known. (3) Unable to act, function, or make progress. (4) Spiritually or physically destroyed. (5) Completely absorbed: rapt<stood by the window, lost in thought>. This is in Webster's II Dictionary.

Twenty-six years later, Mr. Ray Wright, the principal at that time, decided to speak up about the problem concerning Bobby Smith at the high school, felt the need to apologize for what had happened to Bobby and also admitted not doing anything about the problem by turning a cheek from the crime as stated above, not to be in control or good at protecting this student's civil right, which could have been considered the right to an education. At that time, Bobby was at a growing point of his life. Some say that he did that because he was sick and wanted to make peace with his conscience and God before dying. I will never forget the moment that I experienced the racial hatred that someone had in mind for me, words from a human being of authority. "Don't be a smart Northern here" in the educational system because I questioned about my grade, "Why did I get the grade on my project?" They tried to break me down mentally, repeatedly. Going to school in the South, enjoying the education, but the grades were an injustice and will have you change your major for your future. Amazing what people say and do to you to discredit a person or people to stop their growth and goals.

One of my greatest moments of my life was having the opportunity among others was the day, I met Mr. Harry Belafonte. He was invited by the governor and his wife to speak on human and civil rights at the auditorium. After his spoke to a select audience, we were allowed to ask Mr. Belafonte questions. I stood up to ask him, not just coming from the president of the NAACP, but as a person there, "Can you explain to the people what racism is and what was racism like from your perspective?" Mr. Belafonte began, about his experience coming to America. It was very interesting the audience enjoyed the response to my question. Among the group, the majority of Caucasian audience, sometimes a person may not get what it means or what is being said. Afterward at the governor's mansion, there he was, just standing there. We started talking, and somewhere in the conversation he said, "Take the ball and run with it."

For many years, I kept those words close to my soul, because you must believe in something to know where you are going. To think of all the people in the world he'd met, and he would tell me that with good intent. Here's a man that has been around Dr. Martin Luther King, Sidney Poitier, Muhammad Ali, Robert F. Kennedy, Paul Robeson, Nelson Mandela, Ruby Dee, Rosa Park and so many great men and women in Hollywood and around the world.

Even as adults, we forget bullies grow up and become adult bullies in the workplace. Most of the time we work side by side with a bully, who is causing someone a lot of pain on the job now. Looking back at postal office crimes, was the boss the bully, or was the person who brought a gun to work, being bullied, made to feel low, or were they the bully? Many people were fired or being misused in the workplace. We have innocent hardworking people being harassed by others, as in the street crime. In each case, it was because there wasn't anyone caring enough to stand up. Look at the communities dying. School activities values are changing inside because of money and because someone wants to be important, just to rise in position and for money, wanting everything to look perfect on the outside, while someone maybe crying or dying on the inside. Dreams are lost, communities are taken over, and children are lost in the best times of their lives afraid of not knowing if anyone is noticing what is really going on around them. Stop, listen, and look at what is going around the schools, workplace and communities.

Did you think our governmental system, at many levels needs to be refined to work with the common changes of this day in time? The People reflect our government, our schools, and our communities. Most of all, we as a people, are the nation. Something as little as a city park and the roads will tell you about the city in that location and how it is run, under the administration that causes the area to be managed. Is it welcoming us all, if it is a public place? However, something's should not change, keeping the basics of enjoying the keys of life. What is considered a good change or bad change?

Looking back and around, out into at the streets, towns and the world in general, isn't sad to see and know that many children are going through some unbelievable problems? Just take a look around to see if your environment is making sense, as well as how your community is functioning. Is it really a healthy living space for all of us? On a small scale, is it a good change or a bad change to enhance the value of many persons around you, or just you? Big companies are taking out streetlights from the communities, without thoughts of the safety of our children walking home in the dark or going to school in the morning in the dark, which is an issue. What are we living for, just to bring fear to the world and people, making rules that make no sense in the end? Just to start all over, putting people in charge of dismantling, our lives that other countries have mastered and made it to be as a healthy or normal way of life?

Sometimes elections campaign can appear to be considered bullying, so what do you think the people understand is a fair game of life, liberty and justice?

Now the question to you is, can you see or hear that the alarm has been ringing for a long time? We are all human beings no matter how, who, and where we live. Being in pain or having the feeling of joy can be looked in the same way. It depends on what side you are experiencing at that moment. We have the right to live a healthy and joyful life on this earth, in a cultural way.

Wake up. We all own the soul of this earth,
in a wild and wonderful way.
When the Violent Change, People Can Too

As it pertains to school violence, 77% of students are bullied verbally, mentally, and physically. About 8% of eighth graders stay home at least once a month to avoid bullying. Young people who bully are more likely to smoke, drink alcohol, and get into fights. Many young people who bully or have been bullied have been at some point ostracized by others, frequently teased or suffer from depression.

Children who bully are learning to use power and aggression to control and distress others. Children who are victimized become increasingly powerless and find themselves trapped in relationships in which they are being abused.

Bullying is associated with a range of physical and mental health problems, as well as suicide, educational problems, antisocial problems, and relationship problems 20-25% of frequently victimized children report bullying as the reason for missing school. A high risk of suicide thoughts is found among children who have been bullied, who bully others, and who are involved in both roles.

13 killed, 24 injured: Columbine, Colorado
APRIL 20, 1999

HARRIS **KLEBOLD**

Eric Harris and Dylan Klebold, students at Columbine High, opened fire at the school, killing a dozen students and a teacher and causing injury to two dozen others before taking their own lives.

*This is the official sticker for the public and private world of not tolerating bullying any more, anywhere. Place this sticker on your front window or door of your business, school, store, bar, and any place you are not allowing bullying. **Stand up for yourself or someone else's right to enjoy a safe environment to live or to be around.***

RIGHT TO LIVE

To those kids who were bullied, and their lives were taken away, your memories are not lost. For those who are still being bullied, stand strong because help is on the way. You win by knowing you are the better person, the bullies are the ones in pain and have a problem, not you.

Save our children, by hearing their silent cries
Khadijah Muhammad

Steps to seek help or the way to handle Bullying:

What does a bully do?

a) Talk mean to the other person, for their own reasons.
b) Use the other person, as a joke or for their own reasons,
c) Hit or throw things at the other person, to show power.
d) Use words to belittle the other person,
e) Do things to make people, not like the other person,
f) Make up acts or embellish the action to make the other person seem bad,
g) Bring other people in on the actions of not liking and wanting the other person to be around that person that is being bullied.
h) They say, they will do bodily harm to the other person,
i) Making the other person feel very uncomfortable,

j)   Using paper or the internet to bring the other person down,

k)   Profiling the sex, race, religion, language, behavior etc. of the person, so, the bully can bring down their self-esteem, as a joke.

l)   A bully can be in any place or time, school, work, in the community, and

What should you do if you are bullied?

a)   Find a comfort zone; to take notes of what's going on.

b)   Think of someone to talk with, to express what is happening to you, so you may be given some directions on how to handle the problem

c)   Know that your rights may be protected by the law or rules.

d)   Beware that the bully has some problems, sometimes they need professional Attention.

e)   Bullies are all ages, sex, religion, background, and race.

f)   Know that you are not alone, PLEASE HOLD ON.

g)   Never try to beat the bully at his own game, try a more intelligent way.

h)   Everyone doesn't have to know you are afraid, but being afraid, is not bad.

i)   If you know someone being bullied, find someone to tell, that will help.

j)   Don't follow the bully or bully's behavior; you may get in more trouble.

k)   Bullying is a hate crime.

l)   People die from bullying and it hurts a person's soul.

CONCLUSION

Looking back in her life she was very happy that she was able to enjoy the culture of many people, even in my family. Maybe one day the world would see that we are not alone, and it is enough for all of us to grow and find help in each other, one way or another. Why wait for an emergency to grow, have fun by sitting back and people watch, you might find they are just like you in some ways. Only a Bully can explain why they are that way, because each case may be different. She can only say this may give you a clear understanding that you are not alone, and bullying is more common, than you know. Even working on Bobby's case and others, she found herself going through some mean, disturbing situations, that could have made her, give up or question the outcome, but deep inside she knew fighting for justice was right and saving a person's life was meaningful, even those, you may not win them all. Bullying is the beginning of a person showing power over you, but hate crimes are the painful and harmful ways a person or people cross the line, of your liberties to live and be at peace. Now BOTH have led to the same violence of the innocence opportunities of a person's life, goals and dreams.

There are many reasons a bully may think, what they are doing is right, some time it might be, that an adult may have been bullied as a child or a child is bullying an adult. Ever way, a child can grow up to be a Bully adult too. Again, it's not kids to kids all the time. However, adults bully each other too.

This story is dictated my family and friends, that were able to be my rock to handle some unbelievable times, during this case, the State of West Virginia, Education Dept., Governor's office, Senator Rockefeller, Judge O. C. Spaulding and the NAACP, those who have help me work toward a safe environment for all children in or out of school, people that are stopping the bullying, as well as those who are helping the survivor's to move on day by day. Having the curious and opportunity to stand up for your rights, by thinking wisely and safe, but most of all, know you are loved by your family, friends and your new friends waiting to meet you. Remember you have a future waiting on you to continue, this is just a moment to grow stronger and began dreaming of *better days ahead* to ENJOY.

Thank you for reading this story, which may make someone's day or may change someone's life, with a better understanding of BULLYING. Sincerely!

See the facts and research, as you continue to read, share this information with a friend in need and before there is a problem, we need to care, and concern for our fellow man, woman and child. Information is POWER!

Find support in any of the following organization; help others be aware, know that:

"A hurting child, becomes a hurting adult one day, do pay attention".

School/Campus/Workplace/Communities Incidents:
(Since July 18, 1984–2016)

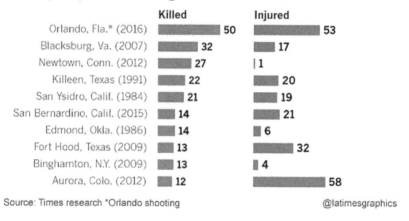

Deadly mass shootings in the U.S.

	Killed	Injured
Orlando, Fla.* (2016)	50	53
Blacksburg, Va. (2007)	32	17
Newtown, Conn. (2012)	27	1
Killeen, Texas (1991)	22	20
San Ysidro, Calif. (1984)	21	19
San Bernardino, Calif. (2015)	14	21
Edmond, Okla. (1986)	14	6
Fort Hood, Texas (2009)	13	32
Binghamton, N.Y. (2009)	13	4
Aurora, Colo. (2012)	12	58

Source: Times research *Orlando shooting   @latimesgraphics

By LOS ANGELES TIMES STAFF
JUNE 12, 2016

"These are becoming common scenes in our lives"

Medical Outlook and Social Reviews

Thought-out this journey of seeing how blind we are as a nation, under one roof called Earth. Man has found it unbelievable to see where we are going, a point of no return, in our communities and family structure, however some people do have it together right under our noses.

Let's look at where our country is at this moment and where we may be in the future. Also, we will look into other crimes, just to show how bad to bad and unsure our front yard have become, that many of us in life are on a tightrope, somewhat not really knowing the person around you in the house, on the job, in the community living in front of you or next to you will be at a point of no return, terrorizing someone else's life, for WHAT?

Now let's look at some facts on Mental illness, studies from the professional side,

Every year, about 42.5 million American adults (or 18.2 percent of the total adult population in the United States) suffers from some mental illness, enduring conditions such as depression, bipolar disorder or schizo-phrenia, statistics released Friday reveal.

The data, compiled by the Substance Abuse and Mental Health Services Administration (SAMHSA), also indicate that approximately 9.3 million adults, or about 4 percent of those Americans ages 18 and up, experience "serious mental illness" that is, their condition impedes day-to-day activities, such as going to work.

The last SAMHSA report, released in 2012, which found that 45.9 million American adults, 20 percent of this demographic, experienced mental illness at least once annually. (Though there is a 1.8 percent difference, the statistics do have margins of error, and methods of compiling them are often revised, so this dip does not necessarily mean there has been a long-term decline in mental illness.)

New Jersey had the lowest rates of overall and severe mental illness, while Utah had the highest. BRIAN SNYDER/REUTERS (NEWSWEEK)

The data, compiled by the **Substance Abuse and Mental Health Services Administration (SAMHSA), in 2014**

The SAMHSA study breaks down mental illness rates by state. Perhaps surprisingly, New Jersey had the lowest national rates of overall and severe mental illness—14.7 percent and 3.1 percent, respectively.

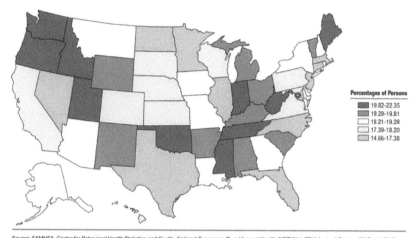

Source: SAMHSA, Center for Behavioral Health Statistics and Quality, National Surveys on Drug Use and Health (NSDUHs), 2011 (revised October 2013) and 2012.

A map of mental illness SAMHSA

The states with the most mental illness?

In Utah, 22.3 percent of the adult population experienced mental illness, and in West Virginia had the most cases of severe mental illness among adults, at 5.5 percent.

It may be tempting to look at the map that accompanies the study and try to make guesses at why, say, the Pacific Northwest and the Midwest seem to suffer more from mental illness than other regions. However, because there is so much mental health illness in all the states and lots of uncontrolled variables it would be hard to draw any real conclusions. According to the study, "factors that potentially contribute to the variation are not well understood and need further study."

I LIKE TO LOOK AT THE DIFFERENCE UNDERSTANDING OF MENTAL ILLNESS TO ALLOW YOU THE READER TO COMPOSE A BETTER UNDERSTANDING FOR YOURSELF, LIKE BEING TAUGHT THROUGH GATHERED INFORMATION I'M ABLE TO GIVE TO YOU IN THIS BOOK, FOR YOU GET A FEEL FOR LONG THE WAY.

Not all psychiatric statisticians are satisfied with SAMHSA's findings, with some alleging that the agency grossly understates the prevalence of mental illness.

Ronald Kessler, McNeil Family Professor of Health Care at Harvard and expert in large scale mental illness surveys, tells Newsweek that SAMHSA's assessment of serious mental illness is "pretty good" but that he believes that the "prevalence for any mental illness is too low."

Kessler, who is familiar with SAMHSA's computational methods, said that the agency did not measure all of the ailments in the Diagnostic and Statistical Manual of Mental Disorders -- including some major ones like attention deficit disorder.

"I find it objectionable that they use this term 'any mental illness,'" he says. "What they really mean is any mental illness that they decided to measure. What they ask about is anxiety and depression and drinking and drugs, but there are many things besides that they totally ignored."

Based on the data even at this time, I wish we the public cause have receive more knowledge would things in our life be done any different, I guess we would just stop, look and listen a little more at our surroundings.

Mental Health Myths and Facts

by MentalHealth.gov

Mental Health Problems Affect Everyone

Myth: Mental health problems don't affect me.

Fact: Mental health problems are actually very common. In 2014, about:

- *One in five American adults experienced a mental health issue*
- *One in 10 young people experienced a period of major depression*
- *One in 25 Americans lived with a serious mental illness, such as schizophrenia, bipolar disorder, or major depression,*

Suicide is the 10th leading cause of death in the United States. It accounts for the loss of more than 41,000 American lives each year, more than double the number of lives lost to homicide.

Myth: Children don't experience mental health problems.

Fact: Even very young children may show early warning signs of mental health concerns. These mental health problems are often clinically diagnosable and can be a product of the interaction of biological, psychological, and social factors.

Half of all mental health disorders show first signs before a person turns 14 years old, and three quarters of mental health disorders begin before age 24.

Unfortunately, less than 20% of children and adolescents with diagnosable mental health problems receive the treatment they need. Early mental health support can help a child before problems interfere with other developmental needs.

Myth: People with mental health problems are violent and unpredictable.

Fact: The vast majority of people with mental health problems are no more likely to be violent than anyone else. Most people with mental illness are not violent and only 3%-5% of violent acts can be attributed to individuals living with a serious mental illness. In fact, people with severe mental illnesses are over 10 times more likely to be victims of violent crime than the general population. You probably know someone with a mental health problem and don't even realize it, because many people with mental health problems are highly active and productive members of our communities.

Myth: People with mental health needs, even those who are managing their mental illness, cannot tolerate the stress of holding down a job.

Fact: People with mental health problems are just as productive as other employees. Employers who hire people with mental health problems report good attendance and punctuality as well as motivation, good work, and job tenure on par with or greater than other employees.

When employees with mental health problems receive effective treatment, it can result in:

- *Lower total medical costs*
- *Increased productivity*
- *Lower absenteeism*
- *Decreased disability costs*

Myth: Personality weakness or character flaws cause mental health problems. People with mental health problems can snap out of it if they try hard enough.

Fact: Mental health problems have nothing to do with being lazy or weak and many people need help to get better. Many factors contribute to mental health problems, including:

- *Biological factors, such as genes, physical illness, injury, or brain chemistry*
- *Life experiences, such as trauma or a history of abuse*
- *Family history of mental health problems*

People with mental health problems can get better and many recover completely.

Helping Individuals with Mental Health Problems

Myth: There is no hope for people with mental health problems. Once a friend or family member develops mental health problems, he or she will never recover.

Fact: Studies show that people with mental health problems get better and many recover completely. Recovery refers to the process in which people are able to live, work, learn, and participate fully in their communities. There are more treatments, services, and community support systems than ever before, and they work.

Myth: Therapy and self-help are a waste of time. Why bother when you can just take a pill?

Fact: Treatment for mental health problems varies depending on the individual and could include medication, therapy, or both. Many individuals work with a support system during the healing and recovery process.

Myth: I can't do anything for a person with a mental health problem.

Fact: Friends and loved ones can make a big difference. Only 44% of adults with diagnosable mental health problems and less than 20% of children and adolescents receive needed treatment. Friends and family can be important influences to help someone get the treatment and services they need by:

- *Reaching out and letting them know you are available to help*
- *Helping them access mental health services*
- *Learning and sharing the facts about mental health, especially if you hear something that isn't true*
- *Treating them with respect, just as you would anyone else*
- *Refusing to define them by their diagnosis or using labels such as "crazy"*

Myth: Prevention doesn't work. It is impossible to prevent mental illnesses.

Fact: Prevention of mental, emotional, and behavioral disorders focuses on addressing known risk factors such as exposure to trauma that can affect the chances that children, youth, and young adults will develop mental health problems. Promoting the social-emotional well-being of children and youth leads to:

- Higher overall productivity
- Better educational outcomes
- Lower crime rates
- Stronger economies
- Lower health care costs
- Improved quality of life
- Increased lifespan
- Improved family life

"Reach to your local Mental Health Services and save a Life or two"

AMERICAN PSYCHOLOGICAL ASSOCIATION

Data on behavioral health in the United States

- Mental illness is associated with increased occurrence of chronic diseases such as cardiovascular disease, diabetes, obesity, asthma, epilepsy and cancer. (CDC)
- Mental illness is associated with lower use of medical care, reduced adherence to treatment therapies for chronic diseases and higher risks of adverse health outcomes. (CDC)
- Many people suffer from more than one mental disorder at a given time. Nearly half (45 percent) of those with any mental disorder meet criteria for two or more disorders, with severity strongly related to comorbidity. (NIMH)
- Mental disorders were one of the five most costly conditions in the United States in 2006, with expenditures at $57.5 billion. (AHRQ) (PDF, 615KB)
- Over 8.9 million persons have co-occurring disorders that is, they have both a mental and substance use disorder. (SAMHSA)

Access to Treatment

- Up to one-in-four primary care patients suffer from depression; yet, primary care doctors identify less than one-third (31 percent) of these patients. (AHRQ) (PDF, 615KB)

- Among the 8.9 million adults with any mental illness and a substance use disorder, 44 percent received substance use treatment or mental health treatment in the past year, 13.5 percent received both mental health treatment and substance use treatment and 37.6 percent did not receive any treatment. (SAMHSA)
- Four percent of young adults reported forgoing mental health care in the past year, despite self-reported mental health needs. (AHRQ) (PDF, 615KB)
- People with psychotic disorders and bipolar disorder are 45 percent and 26 percent less likely, respectively, to have a primary care doctor than those without mental disorders. (AHRQ) (PDF, 615KB)

Depression

- Major depressive disorder is the leading cause of disability in the U.S. for ages 15-44. (NIMH)
- Major depressive disorder affects approximately 14.8 million American adults, or about 6.7 percent of the U.S. population age 18 and older in a given year. (NIMH)
- While major depressive disorder can develop at any age, the median age at onset is 32. (NIMH)
- Major depressive disorder is more prevalent in women than in men. (NIMH)

Anxiety

- Approximately 40 million American adults ages 18 and older, or about 18.1 percent of people in this age group in a given year, have an anxiety disorder. (NIMH)
- Anxiety disorders frequently co-occur with depressive disorders or substance abuse.
- (NIMH)

- Nearly three-quarters of those with an anxiety disorder will have their first episode by age 21.5. (NIMH)

Mental Disorders

- Adults with any type of mental illness in the past year: 45.1 million. (SAMHSA)
- Adults with serious mental illness: 11 million. (SAMHSA)
- Published studies report that about 25 percent of all U.S. adults have a mental illness and that nearly 50 percent of U.S. adults will develop at least one mental illness during their lifetime. (CDC)
- Nearly one-fourth of all adult stays in U.S. community hospitals involve depressive, bipolar, schizophrenia and other mental health disorders or substance use-related disorders. (AHRQ) (PDF, 615KB)

Stigmatization

- Most adults with mental health symptoms (78 percent) and without mental health symptoms (89 percent) agreed that treatment can help persons with mental illness lead normal lives. (CDC)
- 57 percent of all adults believed that people are caring and sympathetic to persons with mental illness. (CDC)
- Only 25 percent of adults with mental health symptoms believed that people are caring and sympathetic to persons with mental illness. (CDC)

Data are from government health agencies under the U.S. Department of Health and Human Services.

Bullying—Wikipedia, the free encyclopedia

https://en.wikipedia.org/wiki/**Bullying**

1. Wikipedia

   Definition—There is no universal definition of bullying, however, it is widely agreed upon that bullying is a subcategory of aggressive behavior…

1.

   Bullying definition: a blustering, quarrelsome, overbearing person who habitually badgers and intimidates smaller or weaker people.

Definition of Workplace Bullying | Workplace Bullying Institute

Workplace Bullying is repeated, health-harming mistreatment of one or more persons (the targets) by one or more perpetrators. It is abusive conduct that is: Threatening, humiliating, or intimidating, or. Work interference sabotage which prevents work from getting done, or. Verbal abuse.

Emotional Abuse: Definitions, Signs, Symptoms, Examples...

Emotional abuse is:

"Any act including confinement, isolation, verbal assault, humiliation, intimidation, infantilization, or any other treatment which may diminish the sense of identity, dignity, and self-worth."

What is emotional bullying in schools?

Emotional bullying is a deliberate attempt to hurt someone else, according to the British non-profit parent-support organization Ask Wiltshire. Examples of **emotional bullying** include cruel teasing, talking viciously about people behind their backs, spreading humiliating rumors, and excluding kids from group activities.

"Believe that life is worth living and your belief will help create the fact."—**William James**

Emotional Child Abuse

What Is Emotional Abuse?

Emotional abuse of a child is commonly defined as a pattern of behavior by parents or caregivers that can seriously interfere with a child's cognitive, emotional, psychological or social development. Emotional abuse of a child also referred to as psychological maltreatment can include:

Ignoring. Either physically or psychologically, the parent or caregiver is not present to respond to the child. He or she may not look at the child and may not call the child by name.

Rejecting. This is an active refusal to respond to a child's needs (e.g., refusing to touch a child, denying the needs of a child, ridiculing a child).

Isolating. The parent of caregiver consistently prevents the child from having normal social interactions with peers, family members and adults. This also may include confining the child or limiting the child's freedom of movement.

Exploiting or corrupting.   In this kind of abuse, a child is taught, encouraged or forced to develop inappropriate or illegal behaviors. It may involve self-destructive or antisocial acts of the parent or caregiver, such as teaching a child how to steal or forcing a child into prostitution.

Verbally assaulting.   This involves constantly belittling, shaming, ridiculing or verbally threatening the child.

Terrorizing.   Here, the parent or caregiver threatens or bullies the child and creates a climate of fear for the child. Terrorizing can include placing the child or the child's loved one (such as a sibling, pet or toy) in a dangerous or chaotic situation or placing rigid or unrealistic expectations on the child with threats of harm if they are not met.

Neglecting the child.   This abuse may include educational neglect, where a parent of caregiver fails or refuses to provide the child with necessary educational services; mental health neglect, where the parent or caregiver denies or ignores a child's need for treatment for psychological problems; or medical neglect, where a parent or caregiver denies or ignores a child's need for treatment for medical problems.

Stopping Animal Abuse and Neglect

Anti-cruelty laws vary from state, and sometimes from city to city or county to county. The legal definitions of abuse, neglect or appropriate conditions may differ. The penalties for animal abuse may also differ.

Fortunately, society has begun to recognize animal abuse as part of the cycle of violence and is calling for stronger penalties against abusers and more powerful enforcement capabilities. As a result, many states have added felony penalties to their anti-cruelty laws.

Here are some sure signs of animal neglect:

No Shelter: Animals need protection from the elements while outdoors to ensure their welfare and well-being.

Collar too tight: Not increasing the size of a collar as an animal grows causes injury, strangulation and death.

Lack of grooming: Without regular grooming, a pet, especially a long-haired one, can get massive matting and sores.

Mange: Mange, caused by tiny parasites, leads to itching, loss of hair and sores from scratching and biting to relieve the irritation. Mange is easily treated with medicated baths.

Starvation: Starvation is caused not only by lack of food, but also by improper food, untreated disease and parasites (like worms).

Animal Abuse

It's easier to recognize physical abuse when you see something cruel like choking, setting tails on fire, dunking heads underwater, kicking and hitting.

"No one can make you feel inferior without your consent."—**Eleanor Roosevelt**

"Pets are for comfort and joy, not for you to abuse and your self- esteem, know their worth."—**Khadijah Muhammad**

Look in the box to see if you understand or relate to any problems you or any person you know is going through, it is more easy to see for themselves, unto you're ready to talk about it, do your homework.

iPredator Inc. is a New York State based Internet Safety Company founded in September 2011 to provide educational and advisory products & services to online users and organizations. Their areas of expertise include cyberbullying, cyberstalking, cybercrime, internet defamation, cyber terrorism, online predation, internet addiction and the new fields they are pioneering called Cybercriminal Psychology & Profiling. Created by a NYS licensed psychologist and certified forensic consultant, Michael Nuccitelli Psy.D., their goal is to reduce victimization, theft and disparagement from online assailants.

Dr. Nuccitelli and iPredator Inc. consultants are always available, at no cost, to interact with online users and media. In addition to their professional services, Dr. Nuccitelli has authored a variety of internet safety tools, cyber attack, risk assessments and diagnostic tests available to purchase as hard copy PDF files.

Cyberbullying is bullying that takes place using electronic technology. Electronic technology includes devices and equipment such as cell phones, computers, and tablets as well as communication tools including social media sites, text messages, chat, and websites.

Risk Factors

No single factor puts a child at risk of being bullied or bullying others. Bullying can happen anywhere cities, suburbs, or rural towns. Depending on the environment, some groups such as lesbian, gay, bisexual, or transgendered (LGBT) youth, youth with disabilities, and socially isolated youth may be at an increased risk of being bullied.

Federally Collected Data Reports

The 2011 Youth Risk Behavior Surveillance System (Centers for Disease Control and Prevention) indicates that 20% of students in grades 9–12 experienced bullying nationwide.

The 2008–2009 School Crime Supplement (National Center for Education Statistics and the Bureau of Justice Statistics) indicates that 28% of students in grades 6–12 experienced bullying nationwide.

National Statistics

Been Bullied
28% of U.S. students in grades 6–12 experienced bullying.9
20% of U.S. students in grades 9–12 experienced bullying.10

Bullied Others
Approximately 30% of young people admit to bullying others in surveys.[11]

Seen Bullying
70.6% of young people say they have seen bullying in their schools.[12]

70.4% of school staff have seen bullying. 62% witnessed bullying two or more times in the last month and 41% witness bullying once a week or more.[13]

When bystanders intervene, bullying stops within 10 seconds 57% of the time.[14]

Been Cyberbullied

6% of students in grades 6–12 experienced cyberbullying.[15]

16% of high school students (grades 9–12) were electronically bullied in the past year.[16]

However, 55.2% of LGBT students experienced cyberbullying.[17]

*"A lot of people are afraid to tell the truth, to say no. That's where toughness comes into play. Toughness is not being a bully. It's having backbone."—**Robert Kiyosaki***

Psychological Issues Are Common Effects of Bullying

Victims of bullying commonly demonstrate a number of psychological problems, particularly depression and anxiety. Girls may also develop eating disorders after or while being bullied. In addition, victimized children of both sexes may develop psychosomatic issues, which are bodily complaints that have no physical cause.

For instance, victims often suffer from headaches or stomach aches, particularly before the school day begins.

Effects of Bullying Include Problems with Sleep

Bully victims often have a range of sleep issues. They may have difficulties falling asleep, staying asleep and/or getting their needed rest in any given night. When victims are able to sleep, they are more likely to experience nightmares than their non-victimized peers. These nightmares tend to be vivid and menacing and may or may not involve the bully.

Victims of Bullying May Become Suicidal

Unfortunately, victims of bullying have higher rates of suicidality than their peers. This means that they think about committing suicide much more often than others their age. As many high-profile cases make clear, a number of victims follow through on these suicidal thoughts.

"You will never reach higher ground if you are always pushing others down."—**Jeffrey Benjamin**

"Believe that life is worth living and your belief will help create the fact."—**William James**

While there aren't noticeable gender gaps in the location of bullying, female students were significantly more likely than male students to be made fun of, called names or insulted (14.7 percent compared with 12.6 percent), to be the subject of rumors (17 percent compared with 9.6 percent) and to be excluded from activities on purpose (5.5 percent compared with 3.5 percent). Male students who were bullied were more likely than female students to be pushed, shoved, tripped or spit on (7.4 percent compared with 4.6 percent).

Overall, bullied students were most likely to be made fun of, called names or insulted (13.6 percent) or to be the subject of rumors (13.2 percent). The most common forms of cyberbullying were unwanted contact via text messaging and posting harmful information on the Internet.

Among students who were cyberbullied, female students were more likely to have hurtful information about them posted on the Internet (4.5 percent compared with 1.2 percent), to receive unwanted contact via instant messaging (3.4 percent compared with 1 percent) and unwanted contact via text messaging (4.9 percent compared with 1.6 percent).

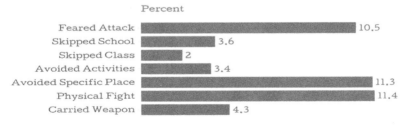

Behavior of Bullied Students
Percent

Feared Attack	10.5
Skipped School	3.6
Skipped Class	2
Avoided Activities	3.4
Avoided Specific Place	11.3
Physical Fight	11.4
Carried Weapon	4.3

USNews   Allie Bidwell for USN&WR; Source: U.S. Department of Education

MORE

Bullying rates are down overall, but female students are still affected more. (ISTOCKPHOTO)

The percentage of students who reported being bullied or cyber-bullied reached a record low in 2013, but female students are still victimized at higher rates, according to new data from the Department of Education.

[READ: High Schooler Forces Cyberbullies to Rethink Their Actions]

The department on Friday released the results of the latest School Crime Supplement to the National Crime Victimization Survey, which showed that in 2013, the percentage of students ages 12-18 who reported being bullied dropped to 21.5 percent. That's down from 27.8 percent in 2011, and a high of 31.7 percent in 2007. The percentage of students who reported being cyberbullied also fell to 6.9 percent in 2013, down from 9 percent in 2011.

"When someone is bullying YOU,
It's become that person's wanting to be noticed
by other,
Sad it's on someone else's expense,
So, know your life means more to others,
No matter how it looks now."

Percentage of students ages 12–18 who reported being bullied at school during the school year, by gender: Selected years, 2005 through 2013

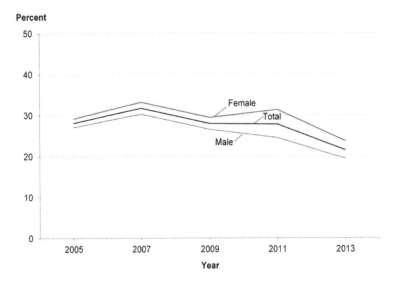

NOTE: "At school" includes the school building, on school property, on a school bus, or going to and from school.

SOURCE: U.S. Department of Justice, Bureau of Justice Statistics, School Crime Supplement (SCS) to the National Crime Victimization Survey, 2005 through 2013.

The percentage of students who reported being bullied dropped to 21.5 percent in 2013, down from a high of 31.7 percent in 2007. COURTESY: U.S. DEPARTMENT OF EDUCATION

The department's National Center on Education Statistics began surveying students on bullying in 2005.

"As schools become safer, students are better able to thrive academically and socially," Education Secretary Arne Duncan said in a statement. "Even though we've come a long way over the past few years in educating the public about the health and educational impacts that bullying can have on students, we still have more work to do to ensure the safety of our nation's children."

Despite the overall drop in bullying and cyberbullying, reporting rates remain low just more than one-third of students who were victims of traditional bullying and fewer than one-quarter of cyberbullying victims reported the incident to an adult, the data show.

Female students also still consistently experience higher-than-average rates of victimization 23.7 percent of female students said they had been bullied in 2013, and 8.6 percent said they had been cyberbullied. By comparison, 19.5 percent and 5.2 percent of male students in 2013 said they had been bullied and cyberbullied, respectively.

[MORE: Social Combat: Bullying Risk Increases With Popularity]

While there aren't noticeable gender gaps in the location of bullying, female students were significantly more likely than male students to be made fun of, called names or insulted (14.7 percent compared with 12.6 percent), to be the subject of rumors (17 percent compared with 9.6 percent) and to be excluded from activities on purpose (5.5 percent compared with 3.5 percent). Male students who were bullied were more likely than female students to be pushed, shoved, tripped or spit on (7.4 percent compared with 4.6 percent).

Overall, bullied students were most likely to be made fun of, called names or insulted (13.6 percent) or to be the subject of rumors (13.2 percent). The most common forms of cyberbullying were unwanted contact via text messaging and posting harmful information on the Internet.

Among students who were cyberbullied, female students were more likely to have hurtful information about them posted on the Internet (4.5 percent compared with 1.2 percent), to receive unwanted contact via instant messaging (3.4 percent compared with 1 percent) and unwanted contact via text messaging (4.9 percent compared with 1.6 percent).

"A person in pain, hurts other people, so understand it's not you"

Behavior of Bullied Students

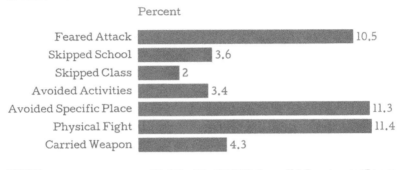

Percent

Feared Attack	10.5
Skipped School	3.6
Skipped Class	2
Avoided Activities	3.4
Avoided Specific Place	11.3
Physical Fight	11.4
Carried Weapon	4.3

Allie Bidwell for USN&WR: Source: U.S. Department of Education

Students who reported being bullied in school were more likely to avoid specific places and engage in a physical fight. ALLIE BIDWELL FOR US NeWS; SOURCE: U.S. DEPARTMENT OF EDUCATION.

Behavior of Cyber-Bullied Students

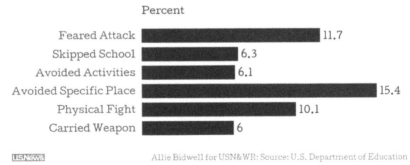

Percent

Feared Attack	11.7
Skipped School	6.3
Avoided Activities	6.1
Avoided Specific Place	15.4
Physical Fight	10.1
Carried Weapon	6

Allie Bidwell for USN&WR: Source: U.S. Department of Education

Students who were cyberbullied more frequently reported bringing a weapon to school. ALLIE BIDWELL FOR US NeWS; SOURCE: U.S. DEPARTMENT OF EDUCATION.

Traditional bullying and cyberbullying also impact the behaviors of the affected students.

Among students who were victims of traditional bullying, more than 1 in 10 said they feared being attacked or harmed at school. That fear was slightly more frequent among victims of cyberbullying: about 1 in 8 students who had been cyberbullied said they feared attack or harm at school.

3 Tips for Parents to Help Their Bullied Kids

Parents should know the signs, introduce a new hobby, and confront the school if needed. Laura McMullen | Staff Writer Feb. 15, 2012,

Kenton Raiford, who was bullied in middle school, now witnesses a lot of bullying in his senior year at Jesse Bethel High School in Vallejo, Calif. While bullies get physical sometimes, he says, "It's more about mental and emotional attacks."

1. Recognize the warning signs: Evidence of bullying isn't usually as obvious as a black eye or broken nose, mostly because, as Raiford says, bullying often takes the shape of verbal abuse

2. Introduce a new hobby: "Find something that your child has a passion for and an interest in, and get him to focus on that," says Raiford. "He'll find other people that he can connect with people who have that same passion and drive."

3. Work with the school: If parents suspect their child is being bullied, they need to work collaboratively with the school to stop the bully.

Some Definitions for different forms of BULLYING

By ipredator.org

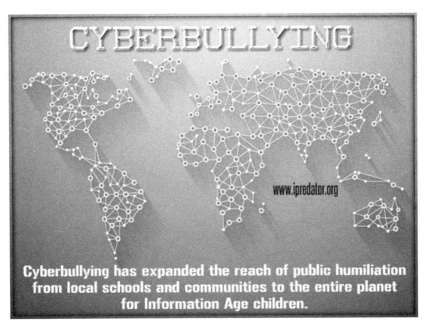

By www.ipredator.org

Bash Boards

Bash Boards: Bash Boards are a cyberbullying tactic describing a case of cyber-attacks a cyberbully initiates in chat rooms, "virtual" rooms, online forums and message boards. Within these social exchange sites, children disseminate and exchange information they deem important, socially relevant or noteworthy for their peers to view, comment on and share with other peers. These forums are naturally frequented by cyberbullies and affiliated school acquaintances. The reason they give the slang term of Bash Boards is because cyberbullies or any child can post negative and defamatory information about another child that is public for all to read and shared among forum participants.

Blogobullying

BlogoBullying: BlogoBullying is a cyberbullying tactic describing when a cyberbully creates a blog with the target child being the central subject and topic of blog posts. Although BlogoBullying is the least frequently used tactic in a cyberbullies cyber attack toolbox, it is by far the most content rich method and can cause long-term injury to the target child when applying for employment and college admissions. Not only does BlogoBullying include defamatory, felonious and humiliating information about the target minor, but with a universal understanding of search engine optimization (SEO) by the cyberbully, their derogatory laden posts can page rank on the first page of Google.

Cyberbullying by Proxy

Cyberbullying by Proxy: Cyberbullying by Proxy is a cyberbullying tactic describing a cyberbully who encourages, deceives or persuades other online users to harass a target child. Cyberbullying by proxy is a dangerous kind of cyberbullying in that adults may become accomplices to the cyberbully. For many adult accomplices who are rigged by the primary cyberbully, they do not recognize they are abusing a minor or possibly a child of someone they know. With cyberbullying by proxy, the primary cyberbully will go to any lengths to incite counter attacks and retaliation against the target child. To control others into attacking the target child, cyberbullies use other common tactics to take on their malevolent objectives.

Cyberstalking

Cyberstalking: Cyberstalking is a cyberbullying tactic that some internet safety professionals feel should not be included with cyberbullying when abiding by the conventional definition of cyberstalking. When hanging on the softer side of the severity spectrum, cyberstalking may be categorized as a cyberbullying tactic when it includes intimidation, vilification and persistent taunting delivered via Information and Communications Technology channels that do not prioritize threatening the target child's physical safety. Furthermore, it is acceptable to include cyberstalking as a cyberbullying tactic when the cyberbullies methods are not resoundingly communicating physical threats against the target child or anyone the target child is dependent upon in their daily lives.

Cyber Drama

Cyber Drama: Cyber Drama is a cyberbullying tactic that is a lot more common than moderate to extreme cases of cyberbullying. Cyber Drama tends to be mild cyberbullying or gossip that was not thought to be shared on a social or a "flame war" that terminates after a few messages. Most child and adolescent online users are perceptive about telling each other to refrain and will block a user or open a new account when necessary. Some children engaged in Cyber Drama can be psychologically affected due to their negative perception of the data being passed around. Cyber Drama is best identified as a passive aggressive kind of cyberbullying.

Cyber Harassment

Cyber Harassment: Cyber Harassment is a cyberbullying tactic that describes the sending of hurtful defamatory messages to a target child that is worded in a severe, persistent or pervasive manner. When persistent and disparaging, Cyber Harassment can cause the target child significant distress and undue worry. These threatening messages are hurtful, frequent and very dangerous. Like the adult form of cyber harassment, this cyberbullying tactic requires three or more harassing messages related by the theme of the message sent. As a cyberbullying tactic, Cyber Harassment is both negative in content and frequent in communication.

Cyber Threats

Cyber Threats: Cyber Threats are a cyberbullying tactic whereby a cyberbully actively engaged in passive aggressive strategies of informing the target child that he or she is in danger from unknown or felonious assailants. Although the term, Cyber Threats, is often equated with Cyber Terrorism, this cyberbullying tactic is based in using threatening or fear provoking information to frighten the target child. The cyberbully who is informing the target child is rarely the alleged child planning the assault. Given the goal of the cyberbully is to inspire fear in the target child, some cyberbullies will feign suicidal ideations and plans to cause the target child tremendous fear.

Denigration

Denigration: Used in both classic and cyberbullying, "denigration" is a term describing when cyberbullies send, post, or publishes cruel rumors, gossip and false assertions about a target child intentionally damaging their reputation or friendships. Also known as "dissing", this cyberbullying method is a common element and layer involved in most all of the cyberbullying tactics listed. The main goal of Denigration is to humiliate & disparage the target child.

Digital Piracy Inclusion

Digital Piracy Inclusion: Digital or Internet Piracy is broadly defined as the illegal reproduction and distribution of copyrighted material on the internet using Information and Communications Technology. Although most cyberbullies do not fully understand the legal and criminal implications related to Digital Piracy, they are succinctly aware that it is an online behavior to avoid. As a cyberbullying tactic, the cyberbully encourages the target child to engage in Digital Piracy and then reports them to the authorities, their parents or educators.

eIntimidation

eIntimidation: eIntimidation is a colloquial expression describing a cyberbully tactic used to inspire fear in the target child by communicating threats that may be direct or implied using email as the vehicle of communication. Upon emailing the target child their threat, the cyberbully also informs other members in the peer group of the alleged threat. The cyberbully sends a threatening email to the target child and then forwards or copies and pastes the threatening message to others of the implied menace. If these threats at once or indirectly suggest physical harm, they proceed to the tactic of cyberstalking.

Exclusion

Exclusion (aka, Social Exclusion): Exclusion is a cyberbullying tactic that is highly effective and directly targets a child's developmental need to feel accepted and part of a social construct. Social exclusion occurs by indirectly sending a harmful message to the target child that they are not included in social activities without the need for verbal deprecation. As it is well-known children and teens are developmentally fixated being recognized by their peers; the process of designating who is a member of the peer group and who is not included can be devastating to the target child.

Exposure

Exposure: Exposure is a cyberbullying tactic that includes the public display, posting or forwarding of personal communication, images or video by the cyberbully that is personal and private to the target child. Exposure becomes even more detrimental to the target child when the communications posted and displayed publicly contains sensitive personal information or images and video that are sexual in nature. As mobile device technology, images and video becomes more commonplace, the tactic of Exposure is certain to become prevalent.

CYBERBULLY MIND

The Cyberbully Mind is a brief introduction to the psychodynamics of cyberbullying. Cyberbullying is defined as the use of Information and Communication Technology (ICT), by a minor, to verbally and/or physically attack another minor, who is unable or unwilling to deescalate the engagement. Given that the vast majority of this abuse occurs in cyberspace, the factors, drives and motivations for cyberbullying are explored.

Instant Messaging Attacks

Instant Messaging Attacks: Instant Messaging is a type of communications service that enables online users to create a private chat room with another individual. Cyberbullies use IM to send harassing and threatening messages to the target child themed with disparaging information. IM has become a very big portion of the social life of child and adolescent online users. The conversations and conflicts that arise online often give rise to behaviors that are acted out in person during school or at the local shopping mall.

Mobile Device Image Sharing

Mobile Device Image Sharing: Not just a tactic used in cyberbullying, but a pattern of information exchange that can be a criminal act if the pictures are pornographic or graphic enough depicting under aged children. Children can receive images directly on their phones and then send them to everyone in their address books. Some children actually post these images on video sites, their social networking profiles and other programs for anyone to download or view. With the development and widespread usage of mobile device technology, this cyberbullying tactic will become dominant.

Password Theft & Lockout

Password Theft & Lockout: A cyberbully steals the target child's password and begins to chat with other people, pretending to be the target child (a.k.a. Impersonation.) Confident that others think he/she is the target child, they begin to communicate provocative and adversarial messages that are offensive and anger the target child's friends or strangers. In addition to impersonating the target child, the cyberbully locks out the target child from his/her accounts by changing his/her password. Witho ut having access to his/her username or email account, the target child is unable to shut down or prove he/she is not the culprit spreading the vitriolic information.

Phishing

Phishing: Phishing is a cyberbully tactic that requires tricking, persuading or manipulating the target child into revealing personal and/or financial information about themselves and/or their loved ones. Once the cyberbully acquires this information, they begin to use the information to access their profiles if it may be the target child's password. Phishing, also includes purchasing unauthorized items with the target child's or parents' credit cards.

Warning Wars

Warning Wars: Internet Service Providers (ISP) offer a way for consumers to report an online user who is posting inappropriate or abusive information. As a tactic used in cyberbullying and harassment, children engage in "warning wars" by making false allegations to the ISP regarding the target child posting inappropriate information. By doing this frequently enough, often times the target child has their profile and/or account suspended by the ISP. Concurrent with this tactic, the cyberbully informs the target child's parents causing additional admonishment.

Web Page Assassination

Web Page Assassination: This is a tactic whereby the cyberbully creates websites that insult or endanger the target child. The cyberbully creates, designs, and posts web pages specifically designed to insult the target child, their peers or groups of people who share similar characteristics as the target child such as their race, religion or sexual orientation. Although website creation has become an easy task with contemporary information technology software, many cyberbullies have acquired skills enabling them to create websites that are both appealing to viewers but presenting the target child in a negative light.

> *"The Information Age technocentric concept of being "connected" is a paradox of disconnection causing us to lose control of our instinctual drives for social cohesion, allegiance and selflessness. As our dependency upon Information and Communications Technology (ICT) grows, spreading throughout our collective human consciousness, the less we care for our neighbors and the more we delude ourselves into thinking that online connections are far more valuable than reality-based relationships."* Michael Nuccitelli, Psy.D. (2014)

> *"Never be bullied into silence. Never allow yourself to be made a victim. Accept no one's definition of your life but define yourself."*—**Tim Fields**

International Journal of NEUROPSYCHOTHERAPY (IJNPT)

This form of online journalist, is sharing quality research in the fields of Interpersonal Neurobiology, Neuroscience and Brain – based therapies. Focusing on the roots in neurobiology and psychotherapy stretching back towards the twentieth century and the origins of modern neuroscience and psychotherapy.

The first edition, was written by Peter Rossouw, Ph.D., The University of Queensland, Brisbane, Australia, Mediros Clinic Solutions, Brisbane, Australia and Unit for Neuropsychotherapy, Brisbane, Australia.

Bullying is a widely used term that is mostly linked to some form of harassment-be it emotional, verbal or physical. These definitions always refer to specific behaviors (the perpetrator perspective) and the emotional and physical harm they inflict (the victim perspective). Although some definitions of bullying refer to physical harm as one consequence, it is noteworthy that no definition specifically refers to neural changes, despite a large body of evidence that shows the detrimental effects on neurochemical production, changes in neural functioning, and neural damage.

There are some explores definitions of bullying and key neurobiological marker linked to bullying, which are:

    a.   The neurodevelopmental indicators (genetic markers)
    b.   Neurochemical markers
    c.   Neuro-structural markers

Summary

Bullying informs various aspects of the – it changes neurochemical activation, inhibits neural proliferation and causes neuro-structural changes. These changes set a new trajectory of neural functioning and provide the basis for changes in mood, cognition and behaviors. Recent

Recent developments in neuroscience provide the platform for assessing bullying from a neural perspective. It also provides a platform for assessing the efficacy of interventions. In any definition of bullying, the neural impact on victims needs to be considered.

Rossouw, P.J. (2012), Bullying: A Neurobiological Perspective, Neuropsychotherapy in Australia 15:3-9.

Stopbullying.gov

Bullying often includes:

    a.   Teasing
    b.   Talking about hurting someone
    c.   Spreading rumors
    d.   Leaving kids out on purpose
    e.   Attacking someone by hitting them or yelling at them

Kids who are bullied can feel like they are:

    a.   Different
    b.   Powerless
    c.   Unpopular
    d.   Alone

Kids who are bullied have a hard time standing up for themselves. They think the kid who bullies them is more powerful than they are. Bullying can make them:

    a.   Sad, lonely, or nervous
    b.   Feel sick
    c.   Have problems at school

    d.   Bully other kids

Kids bully others for many reasons, they may:
    a.   Want to copy their friends
    b.   Think bullying will help them fit in
    c.   Think they are better than the kid they are bullying

STREET HARASSMENT AND THE LAW

Street Harassment and the Law

Did you know that many forms of street harassment are illegal in the United States, and you can report them to the police?

Reasons to Report

* It can give you a sense of justice and empowerment.
* It may prevent future acts of harassment or more severe crimes.
* It can help raise awareness about how upsetting and inappropriate street harassment really is.

When to Report

You can report an act of street harassment as it happens, by calling 911 on the scene, or after the incident.

* The chances that a street harasser will be apprehended are greatest during and immediately after the incident.

* But if you decide later that something should be reported, you can still call your local

What to Report

To make reporting easier—and to increase the chances that police take you seriously—on each state page we've provided the names of each crime that applies to street harassment so that you can give police the most exact information possible. For example, you can say, "I'd like to report someone for disorderly conduct," or "sexual battery."

If you do report an incident of street harassment or think you might want to report it later, it helps to:

* Make sure you're safe before you do anything else.
* Take a deep breath. Try to stay calm. Street harassment is never your fault, and you're doing the right thing.
* If the crime you're reporting is in progress, call 911. If it has already happened, call your local non-emergency number.
* Ask anyone who saw the incident whether a friend or a stranger if s/he would be willing to serve as a witness for the police. Take down his or her contact information and include it in your report.
* Write down everything you remember, including the time and place of the incident, what the harasser did and said, and a physical description of the harasser (eye color, hair color, approximate height and build, age, etc.). Details can fade from your mind quickly, so even if you aren't sure you'll report something, it's a good idea to make thorough notes of what happened.
* If you do speak to an officer, try not to be intimidated. It's his or her job to ask you a lot of questions. Do your best to answer them and know that you can always follow up with more information later.

* If an officer does ask what *you* were wearing, why you were out alone, or another irrelevant or victim-blaming question, it's ok to (politely) say, "I don't think that's relevant, sir/ma'am. The harasser was wearing…"
* Also, it's important to note that many states have provisions that punish repeated behavior more severely. You may not know when a street harasser is a repeat offender or is about to become one.
* Many states also punish street harassment and sexual harassment more severely if the offender is a government employee or the victim is a minor.
* If you are under 18 or you witness harassment of a young person or child, this is important information to report to the police.

Stop Street Harassment   P.O. Box 3621   Reston, VA 20195

Blue Lives Matter, All Lives Matter

"Remember to Look and Think about the public, not only as criminals, but as humans too."

Khadijah Tiya Muhammad

You're allowed to scream,

you're allowed to cry,

but do not give up.

HPLVRJKZ.COM

Ψ

Listening to
5 to 10 songs a day
can improve
memory, strengthen
immune system and
reduce depression
risk by 80%.

THEPSYCHMIND.COM

Police Abuse and Bullying = Harassment

Police Abuse and Harassment, does it lead to death

In Ferguson and the broader *St. Louis region*, the St. Louis region below you will see Ferguson Cop Darren Wilson and Michael Brown Jr., 18 years old on August 9, 2014, was killed in a shooting by Wilson.

Kate Abbey-Lambertz National Reporter, The Huffington Post

Miriam Carey's mother, Idella Carey, and Charles Barron protest Carey's death on the West Front of the Capitol, October 3, 2014. Tom Williams/CQ Roll Call

U.S. Secret Service and Capitol Police officers fatally shot Miriam Carey in a car chase after she drove her car into a security checkpoint near the White House, refusing orders to stop. Officers fired multiple shots at Carey, a dental hygienist from *Connecticut*, hitting her five times. Her 1-year-old daughter was in the car at the time and survived.

Tanisha Anderson, Died Nov. 13, 2014, age 37, *Cleveland, Ohio*

A medical examiner ruled Anderson's death a homicide, the result of being "physically restrained in a prone position by Cleveland police." Her heart condition and bipolar disorder were also considered factors. The 37-year-old died in November after her mother called 911 while Anderson was having a "mental health episode." Officials say when officers tried to take Anderson to a treatment facility, to undergo a psychiatric evaluation.

On April 12, 2015, **Freddie Carlos Gray, Jr., a 25-year-old**, African American man was arrested by *Baltimore* Police Department for possessing an illegal switchblade, stated by the police. While being transported in the police van, Gray fell into a coma and was taken to a trauma center. Gray died on April 19, 2015; his death was ascribed to injuries to his spinal cord.

The *Cleveland Ohio* Police shot and killed **Tamir Rica, 12 year old**, African American boy in the Cudell Recreation Center, on November 22, 2014, police responded to the police dispatch call "of a male black sitting on the swing and pointing a gun at random people in the city park", two police officers responded, Timothy Loehmann and Frank Garmback.

People Killed by Police in the US in 2016

Showing the frequency of people killed by police per one million of that race's population

Native American.......................3.4 per Million
Black.............................3.23 per Million
Hispanic/Latino................1.51 per Million
White........................1.35 per Million
Asian/Pacific Islander......0.5 per Million

Source: The Counted. As of July 7, 2016

In St. PAUL, Minn., **Philando Castile age 32**, July 7, 20016 (Reuters)—A police officer fatally shot a black man during a traffic stop near *Minneapolis* and the victim's girlfriend posted live footage of the bloody aftermath to Facebook, sparking immediate outrage and a call by the state governor for a federal investigation. "Police officers should not be able to gun a man down for no reason," Diamond Reynolds, the girlfriend of shooting victim Philando Castile, told reporters and sympathizers on Thursday, hours after the Wednesday evening incident.

The governor's assertion appeared validated by a report that Minnesota police stopped Castile a staggering 52 times in the last 14 years.

Police gave no medical attention to the dying Castile as he bled out, victim Philando Castile
(LAVISH REYNOLDS VIA FACEBOOK)

On July 6, 2016, **Alton Sterling**, the **37-year-old** man who was fatally shot by police on video after selling CDs, was a regular presence at the *Baton Rouge, La.*, store where he died known to locals as "CD man." Sterling was the father of five children. One of them, 15-year-old Cameron Sterling, broke down in tears during a family news conference while standing by his mother, Quinyetta McMillan.

Tarika Wilson died Jan. 4, 2008 at 26 years old, was killed when a Lima Police SWAT team, in Lima, Ohio, raided her rental home to arrest her boyfriend on drug charges, according to The New York Times. She had her youngest son, Sincere, in her arms when she was shot by Sgt. Joseph Chavalia. Sincere, who was 14 months old, was shot in the shoulder and hand but survived.

Aiyana Stanley-Jones, Died May 16, 2010, age 7, Detroit, Michigan

Aiyana Stanley-Jones was sleeping on her couch with her grandmother when police conducted a "no knock" raid of their homes. Officer Joseph Weekley was first through the door and after a flash-bang grenade went off, he fired his gun, killing Aiyana. Weekley testified the grandmother struck his weapon and caused him to fire, but she denies being near the gun.

Trayvon B. Martin, born February 5, 1995, was **a 17-year-old African American** he was 6'3" and a pretty big guy, a high school student who lived in Miami Gardens, Florida with his mother Sybrina Fulton. In February 2012, Martin was visiting his father Tracy Martin in *Sanford, Florida* after receiving a ten-day suspension from Krop Senior High School. The suspension stemmed from the discovery of drug residue in Martin's book bag.

February 26, 2012—George Zimmerman, a neighborhood watch captain in Sanford, Florida, calls 911 to report a suspicious person" in the neighborhood. He is instructed not to get out of his SUV or approach the person. Zimmerman disregards the instructions. Moments later, neighbors report hearing gunfire. Zimmerman acknowledges that he shot Martin, claiming it was in self-defense. In a police report, Officer Timothy Smith writes that Zimmerman was bleeding from the nose and back of the head.

"The list has many names on it, let's save a life, let's save our own, wherever you are, by remembering those names that are gone."

A List of attacks against Gay clubs and events:

PULSE NightClub

Orlando (AFP)—**Fifty people died and another 53 were injured** early Sunday when a heavily armed gunman opened fire and seized hostages at a gay nightclub in Orlando, Florida, police said, in the worst mass shooting in US history, June 12, 2016.

The gunman

The shooter has been identified as Omar Mateen, 29, of Port St. Lucie, Florida., authorities said. Mateen had reportedly made calls to 911 early Sunday stating his allegiance to ISIS. He was first flagged on the FBI's radar in 2013 and then again in 2014, FBI Assistant Special Agent in Charge Ron Hopper said at a news conference. Both investigations were closed after inconclusive interviews.

Gay Pride Parade, Jerusalem, 2015: An ultra-Orthodox Jewish man stabbed six people, killing one, 10 years after attacking participants in the same parade in 2005.

Central Station, Moscow 2014: The Central Station, a large gay nightclub, was forced to close after a string of attacks, including being sprayed with bullets and gassed. It has since reopened in a new location that has bulletproof glass.

DIY Club, Yerevan, Armenia, 2012: The gay-friendly bar was firebombed and spray-painted with swastikas in the same month. "I continue to get threats saying they will burn, kill me and so on," owner Armine Oganezova told the Institute for War & Peace Reporting at the time.

Egyptian defendants in courtroom cage during 2014 trial (Photo courtesy of DT News)

Worldwide, hundreds of people are in prison or awaiting trial for allegedly violating laws that punish those who are born gay, lesbian or bisexual.

The prison sentences that have been imposed range up to nine years, which is actually toward the lower end of punishments that are on the books in the 76-plus countries where homosexuality is currently illegal.

In the past, this blog tried to keep track of individual cases of LGBTI prisoners and defendants, but the number of cases turned out to be too great to continue. Now, the blog will provide an overview of the most repressive countries and, when possible, will update the list with news of arrests that violate the human rights of LGBTI people.

Finding out about specific cases remains difficult, especially in countries without a free press. Even though this list is depressing, it provides only a narrow window into one of many types of injustice affecting lesbian, gay, bisexual, transgender and intersex people, sometimes with fatal results. (See the section "Other injustices facing LGBTI people" below and the separate article "10 nations where the penalty for gay sex is death.")

At present, the most egregious violations of LGBTI peoples' human rights include these countries:

- **Egypt** ("one of the world's biggest jailers of gay men," where LGBTI community leaders estimate that as many as 500 LGBTI people have been sent to prison.)
- **Saudi Arabia** (In one recent year, religious police reportedly arrested and convicted a total of 260 people.)
- **Morocco** (Dozens of trials for same-sex intimacy are cited by LGBTI rights advocates each year, but are rarely reported in the media.)
- **Nigeria** (Dozens of arrests have been reported, but Nigerian media rarely follow up with reports about any subsequent trials).

And possibly:

- **India** (almost 1,500 people were arrested in 2015 under India's colonial-era anti-gay law, but it was unclear how many of those arrests were actually for sexual assault rather than for consensual same-sex relations

Hundreds IMPRISONED FOR HOMOSEXUALITY

CAMEROON
LGBT prisoners often are imprisoned at Yaoundé Central Prison.
(Photo courtesy of Camerpress.com)

Cameroonian law provides for sentences of up to five years for homosexual activity.

Cornelius Fonya: Seized by a mob that took him to police
9 years in prison. Sentenced Nov. 20, 2013.

Police in the coastal city of Limbe arrested Cornelius Fonya on Oct. 29, 2012, on homosexuality charges after a mob seized him and delivered him to the police station. He pleaded not guilty and was unable to raise the money demanded for bail. In 2013, <u>he was sentenced to nine years in prison</u> for having sexual relations with a 19-year-old youth. The usual maximum in Cameroon for same-sex relations is a five-year sentence, but the penalty is doubled for sex with someone between ages 16 and 21.

EGYPT

Egyptian police typically arrest LGBT people on charges of "sexual immorality" or "debauchery," which Egyptian courts have ruled includes consensual homosexual activity.

One of the world's biggest jailers of gay men

Leaders of the underground LGBTI community in Egypt say that their country has become one of the world's biggest jailers of gay men, with as many as 500 behind bars on "morals" charges. The New York Times estimates that "at least 250 lesbian, gay, bisexual and transgender people have been arrested in a quiet crackdown" since 2013.

Some of those arrests made the news and are listed below:

14 unidentified men arrested in gym/sauna

On Oct. 11, 2013, 14 men were arrested for allegedly engaging in gay sex at a gym/sauna in the El-Marg district in northeastern Cairo. No report of their release has been received, so they are included here as still in prison.

4 men sent to prison for 3 to 8 years for 'deviant parties'

A court sentenced four men to up to eight years in prison on April 7, 2014, for practicing homosexuality, a judicial official said. Prosecutors had accused the men of holding "deviant parties" and dressing in women's clothes. Three were sentenced to eight years and the fourth to three years in prison.

3 to 9 years in prison after police raid a party

Ten people were arrested in November 2013 at party in a residential area of the western Cairo suburb known as 6 October City. One male defendant was sentenced to nine years in prison; other male defendants, to three years. One woman was acquitted.

INDIA

Under a colonial-era law from 1861, intercourse between two people "against the order of nature" is punishable by up to 10 years in prison. India's High Court ruled against enforcement of that law in 2009, but the Supreme Court reinstated it in December 2013.

Almost 1,500 people were arrested in 2015 under Section 377, India's colonial-era anti-gay law, but it was unclear how many of those arrested, if any, were involved in consensual same-sex relations. In 2014, a total of 587 people were arrested under Section 377.

IRAN

Iranian law provides for the death penalty in some cases of consensual same-sex relations both for men and women. Overall, Iran imposes the death penalty more often than any other country except China, but it is unclear how often or if it is applied for consensual homosexual activity.

Oct. 9, 2013, arrests in Kermanshah, Iran
(Photo courtesy of Mehr News Agency)

24 reported arrested and detained

Arrests were made Oct. 8, 2013. The 25 people arrested were reportedly blindfolded and taken to an unknown location. Within a few days they were freed on bail to await trial.

Revolutionary guards in Iran's Kermanshah province made at least <u>24 arrests</u> ("dozens") at a birthday party. They claimed that the arrests resulted from a lengthy investigation into a "a network of homosexuals and devil-worshippers." In an update several weeks after the arrests, activist analyst Scott Long noted that "these cases can drag on for years without a hearing." He added, "My guess is that a lot of [the people arrested] have gone into hiding (i.e. moved to other cities) or, since Kermanshah is near the border, crossed into Iraq or even to Turkey to claim refugee status."

MALAWI

Under Malawian law, homosexual activity is punishable by up to 14 years in prison.

3 men serving prison terms of 10 to 14 years

LGBTQI advocates fault police actions

Amon Champyuni, Mathews Bello and Musa Chiwisi were convicted and sentenced in 2011 for violating Malawi's anti-sodomy law. They are now serving sentences ranging from 10 to 14 years. The country's High Court is reviewing the constitutionality of the anti-sodomy law, and Malawi's justice minister has responded by instructing police to stop making arrests for alleged violations of it.

But <u>the three men remain in prison on the basis of the previous convictions while the High Court reviews their cases.</u>

Anwar Ibrahim of Malaysia (Photo via Photobucket.com)

MALAYSIA

Under Malaysian law, a prison sentence of up to 20 years is provided for "intercourse against the order of nature," including homosexual activity.

Opposition politician stymied by prison sentence for sodomy

A Malaysian court in March 2014 sentenced opposition leader Anwar Ibrahim to five years in prison on sodomy charges, overturning an earlier acquittal and ending his hopes of contesting a local election. He was offered asylum abroad, but declined.

MOROCCO

Under Moroccan law, a prison sentence of up to three years is provided for homosexual activity.

Dozens of arrests go unreported in Morocco

Most homosexuality-related trials in Morocco are not publicized. According to an Associated Press account, the Ministry of Justice reported that 81 such trials occurred in 2011. The Moroccan LGBT activist group Kifkif says that more than 5,000 homosexuals have been put on trial since the country's independence in 1956. That's an average of about 86 per year. This blog has not been able to verify those figures.

The LGBT support group <u>Aswat said that it tallied 19 prosecutions</u> on homosexuality charges during the first three months of 2016.

NIGERIA

Nigerian law provides for sentences of up to 14 years for homosexual activity. In parts of northern Nigeria where sharia law applies, the death penalty can be applied for same-sex intercourse between males. A 2014 law provides for prison sentences of 14 years for getting married to a member of the same sex and 10 years for belonging to a gay organization, supporting same-sex marriages, or making a public display of same-sex affection.

Compiling a comprehensive list of people incarcerated for violations of anti-gay laws in Nigeria is currently impossible. Nigerian newspapers typically report arrests and sometimes the opening of trials of LGBT people, but not the outcome of those events.

Arrests linked to the "Same-Sex Marriage Prohibition Law"

A wave of dozens of arrests was reported during an anti-gay frenzy related to the enactment of the so-called Same-Sex Marriage Prohibition Law in early January 2014. That sweeping law provides for 10-year prison sentences for public displays of same-sex affection, belonging to a gay organization, or supporting same-sex marriages. About 32 were reported arrested in southern Nigeria the Christian section of the country. No further information or updates were available. For purposes of this list, half of them are assumed to have been freed without further legal constraints; of the other half, six are assumed to be in prison awaiting trial and 10 freed on bail awaiting trial.

Among the reported cases:

- Nigeria: Feminine man provokes police raid (August 2016)
- Nigeria: Six suspects in court on homosexuality charges (May 2016)
- Arrest reports in Nigeria: 21 in Delta, 2 in Lagos (November 2015)

SAUDI ARABIA

Under sharia law, the death penalty can be imposed for homosexual activity in Saudi Arabia.

News of arrests for homosexuality is rarely reported in Saudi Arabia, but the practice is reportedly common. In one year recently, religious police reportedly <u>arrested and convicted a total of 260 people</u> on homosexuality-related charges, including charges of cross-dressing, wearing make-up and seeking homosexual encounters.

35 arrested at party

Police and security officers of the Commission for the Promotion of Virtue and Prevention of Vice <u>arrested 35 people on April 4, 2014, at a party near Jeddah that was allegedly for homosexuals</u>. No further word of the arrestees has been received. For this list, with some basis in previous incidents, it is presumed that 20 of them remain in prison and 15 were foreigners who were soon deported.

Twitter user sentenced to 3 years
Prison and whipping for seeking men online

In July 2014, <u>a 24-year-old man was sentenced to three years in prison</u> and 450 lashes by a court in Saudi Arabia for using his Twitter account to meet with gay men.

SENEGAL

Under Senegalese law, a prison sentence of one to five years is provided for homosexual activity.

Journalist's partner imprisoned for gay sex
The more famous of the pair was released

Matar Diop Diagne, the partner of noted journalist Tamsir Jupiter Ndiaye, was <u>convicted of committing "acts against nature" and sentenced to a three-year prison sentence without parole</u> in October 2012. Ndiaye received a four-year prison sentence for gay sex and assault on Diagne, but was released after 14 months. <u>Diagne remained in prison, while Senegalese journalists wondered why he had been forgotten</u> and speculated that he would be released before long.

UGANDA

Ugandan law provides for up to a life sentence for same-sex intercourse. (The new Anti-Homosexuality Act of 2014, before it was overturned, also provided for a life sentence for anyone who "touches another person with the intention of committing the act of homosexuality." That law also provided for sentences of five to seven years for "promoting homosexuality" and for any action that "in any way abets homosexuality and related practices.")

HOW YOU CAN HELP
Here are some ways to give a boost to the struggle to release these prisoners and to repeal all anti-homosexuality laws:

- Support Amnesty International, which campaigns for some LGBT prisoners, most recently Jean-Claude Roger Mbede in Cameroon and Philip Mubiana and James Mwape in Zambia.
- Donate to the St. Paul's Foundation for International Reconciliation, which seeks the repeal of anti-homosexuality laws currently on the books in 76-plus countries.
- Sign online petitions for the release of LGBTI prisoners at allout.org.

Readers, please suggest other steps to take.

OTHER INJUSTICES FACING LGBTI PEOPLE
Of necessity, the lists above omit many types of injustices that confront LGBTI people worldwide. Here are a few of the omissions:

The lists above do not include people who were executed in one of the seven countries where homosexual activity is a capital crime. (In Iran, three people were executed in 2011 for homosexual activities, according to Amnesty International.)

The lists do not include the dozens of gay men who reportedly have been killed by death squads in Iraq without any government interference and sometimes with help from police.

The lists do not include the many people who die of AIDS each year in countries where LGBTI people are excluded from HIV prevention programs. Nor do they include the countless heterosexual women who die of AIDS after contracting HIV from their closeted gay or bisexual husband in countries where homosexuals are stigmatized.

Matthew Shepard, who was killed in 1998, apparently because he was gay. (Photo courtesy of Wikipedia)

The lists do not include lesbians and gays, such as Tyler Clementi of Rutgers University in the United States, who commit suicide because of the scorn they suffer or the unwarranted shame they feel because of who they are.

The lists do not include people <u>killed by bigots</u> because they are gay, such as Matthew Shepard in the United States in 1998, and an alleged 249 people in Peru during 2006-2010.

They do not include people killed because they are working for gay rights, such as Daniel Zamudio in Chile and Thapelo Makutle in South Africa in 2012 and perhaps David Kato in Uganda in 2011.

They also do not include lesbian and bisexual women who suffer "corrective rapes" or sexual assaults because of their sexual orientation.

76+ COUNTRIES WHERE HOMOSEXUALITY IS ILLEGAL

"To those who are lesbian, gay, bisexual or transgender, let me say: You are not alone. Your struggle for an end to violence and discrimination is a shared struggle."—U.N. Secretary-General Ban Ki-moon

Domestic Violence

Understanding Abuse

What is domestic violence?

The University of Michigan defines domestic violence as follows:

Domestic violence occurs when a person uses physical violence, coercion, threats, intimidation, isolation, stalking, emotional abuse, sexual abuse or economic abuse to control another partner in a relationship. Domestic violence can be a single act or a pattern of behavior in relationships, which encompass dating, marriage, family and roommate relationships.

It is a violation of the right we all have to healthy, supportive and safe relationships.

Other definitions:

Survivor: the individual who is being targeted for abuse.

Abuser: the individual who is inflicting the abuse.

Why is the issue of domestic violence important?

Domestic violence is a serious social problem and a national health concern with significant negative impacts on individuals and our communities. It is a primary cause of injury to women in the United States. According to the National Institute of Justice, over one third (37%) of women admitted to an emergency room for violence-related injuries were abused by an intimate partner. Additionally, one in three women in the United States are physically abused by a partner at some point in their lives. The Center for Disease Control reports that approximately 1.3 million women are physically abused each year in the United States.

Domestic violence is illegal

Just as the use of physical violence on the street is illegal, the use of physical violence in a relationship is an illegal act for which the abuser can be arrested and prosecuted.

How does it happen?

If violence or threat of violence has happened more than once or twice, it is extremely likely to happen again. The violence usually gets worse over time, increasing in both frequency and severity. It is common for the abuse to develop into a pattern or cycle of abuse.

- There is a build-up of tensions and a breakdown in communication
- A trigger occurs that sets off the batterer
- A violent event occurs
- The "honeymoon" period follows. The batterer apologizes, asks forgiveness, and swears it will never happen again. He "courts" the partner. The survivor wants to believe the batterer will change and they make up
- Life returns to "normal" until tensions begin again, and the cycle continues

All kinds of people: Domestic violence occurs among all ethnic groups and all cultures, among all ages, all income levels, all faiths and all education levels. For some people, their social, economic or cultural background may make it harder for them to get help. Lack of money, racial bias, language barriers, immigration status, anti-gay or lesbian beliefs, and religious beliefs can create barriers for survivors.

National Domestic Violence hotline
1-800-799-SAFE

Blight and Abandonment
(Housing and Environment Living Conditions)

Around the world humans are living in poor conditions, some more than others, some would call this Injustice for our government to know this and not help or are the People living this way allowing themselves to be a part of the problem, by accepting it. WHY IS THIS WHEN THERE ARE SO MANY HOMELESS PEOPLE LYING AROUND GOING TO WASTE, FEELING HOPELESS AND ABANDONED?

- Synonyms: abandoned property (buildings, lots, real estate), distressed property (buildings, real estate), vacant property (buildings, lots, real estate)
- Broader: blight, urban decay

John F. Kennedy was inaugurated as the 35th president of the United States on the steps of the Capitol in Washington, D.C. in 1961.

John F Kenny said, *"Too often we... enjoy the comfort of opinion without the discomfort of thought."*

"Our problems are man-made; therefore, they may be solved by man. And man can be as big as he wants. No problem of human destiny is beyond human beings."

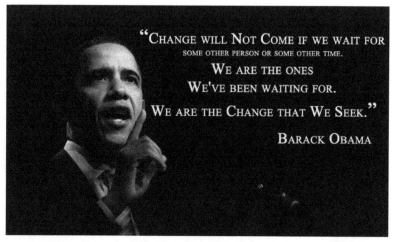

President Barack Obama, of the United States of American, has been in office for 8 years, Jan. 2009-2017

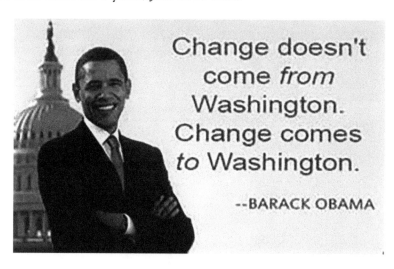

The FBI Federal Bureau
of Investigation

Human Trafficking by FBI

Here in this country, people are being bought, sold, and smuggled like modern-day slaves, often beaten, starved, and forced to work as prostitutes or to take jobs as migrant, domestic, restaurant, or factory workers with little or no pay. Over the past decade, human trafficking has been identified as a heinous crime which exploits the most vulnerable in society. Among the Civil Rights Unit's priorities is its human trafficking program, based on the passage of the 13th Amendment to the U.S. Constitution, which provided that "neither slavery nor involuntary servitude, except as a punishment for crime whereof the party shall have been duly convicted, shall exist within the United States."

Under its human trafficking program, the Bureau investigates matters where a person was induced to engage in commercial sex acts through force, fraud, or coercion, or to perform any labor or service through force, coercion, or threat of law or legal process. Typically, human trafficking cases fall under the following investigative areas:

- *Domestic Sex Trafficking of Adults:* When persons are compelled to engage in commercial sex acts through means of force, fraud, and/or coercion.
- *Sex Trafficking of International Adults and Children:* When foreign nationals, both adult and juveniles, are compelled

to engage in commercial sex acts with a nexus to the United States through force, fraud, and/or coercion. (Note: Matters of domestic juvenile sex trafficking are handled by the FBI's Violent Crimes against Children Section."

- *Forced Labor:* When persons, domestic or foreign nationals, are compelled to work in some service or industry through force or coercion.
- *Domestic Servitude:* When persons, domestic or foreign nationals, are compelled to engage in domestic work for families or households, through means of force or coercion.

Human trafficking task forces

The most effective way to investigate human trafficking is through a collaborative, multi-agency approach with our federal, state, local, and tribal partners. In concert with this concept, FBI investigators participate or lead task forces and working groups in every state within the U.S.

Key Civil Rights Links

Civil Rights Home
Priority Issues
—Hate Crimes
—Human Trafficking/Involuntary Servitude
—Color of Law Violations
—Freedom of Access to Clinic Entrances
—International Human Rights
Report Civil Rights Violations
—Contact your Local FBI Office
—Submit a Tip

Report Trafficking & Get Help

If you believe you are the victim of a trafficking situation or may have information about a potential trafficking situation, call the National Human Trafficking Resource Center (NHTRC) at 1-888-373-7888. NHTRC is a national, toll-free hotline, with specialists available to answer calls from anywhere in the country, 24 hours a day, seven days a week, every day of the year related to potential trafficking victims, suspicious behaviors, and/or locations where trafficking is suspected to occur. You can also submit a tip to the NHTRC **online**.

What Is the Extent of Human Trafficking in the United States?

Contrary to a common assumption, human trafficking
is not just a problem in other countries. Cases of
human trafficking have been reported in all 50 states,
Washington D.C., and some U.S. territories.

Child Trafficking-Human trafficking of children

Victims of human trafficking can be children or adults, U.S. citizens
or foreign nationals, male or female. According to U.S. government
estimates, thousands of men, women, and children are trafficked to
the United States for the purposes of sexual and labor exploitation.

An unknown number of U.S. citizens and legal residents
are trafficked within the country primarily for sexual
servitude and, to a lesser extent, forced labor.

Sex traffickers target children because of their vulnerability and
gullibility, as well as the market demand for young victims.

Those who recruit minors into prostitution violate federal
anti-trafficking laws, even if there is no coercion or movement across
state lines. The children at risk are not just high school students—
studies demonstrate that pimps prey on victims as young as 12.
Traffickers have been reported targeting their minor victims through
telephone chat-lines, clubs, on the street, through friends, and at
malls, as well as using girls to recruit other girls at schools and after-
school programs?

**National 24/7 toll-free Human Trafficking Resource Center
at 1-888-373-7888.**

Trafficking in children (child trafficking) is a global problem affecting large numbers of children. Some estimates have as many as 1.2 million children being trafficked every year.

There is a demand for trafficked children as cheap labor or for sexual exploitation. Children and their families are often unaware of the dangers of trafficking, believing that better employment and lives lie in other countries.

Child trafficking is lucrative and linked with criminal activity and corruption. It is often hidden and hard to address. Trafficking always violates the child's right to grow up in a family environment. In addition, children who have been trafficked face a range of dangers, including violence and sexual abuse. Trafficked children are even arrested and detained as illegal aliens.

"Although our primary focus is on domestic human trafficking, child trafficking in the United States and North America, we also want to help make a global impact in some of the worst nations where this crime is all too accepted as status quo! – Marion Williams, Human Trafficking Movie Project."

Buy Human Trafficking Movie *A Dance For Bethany*

Examples:

FOR IMMEDIATE RELEASE
Monday, June 27, 2016

Leader of Human Trafficking Organization Sentenced to Over 15 Years for Exploiting Guatemalan Migrants at Ohio Egg Farms

FOR IMMEDIATE RELEASE
Wednesday, June 29, 2016

Vinton Man Sentenced on Sex Trafficking Charges

Terrell Banker to Serve 156 Months in Federal Prison

FOR IMMEDIATE RELEASE
Wednesday, July 6, 2016

Brooklyn, New York Man Pleads Guilty To Sex Trafficking And Drug Distribution

FOR IMMEDIATE RELEASE
Friday, July 8, 2016

Middle District Of Louisiana Human-Trafficking Task Force Investigation Results In Indictment For Child Sex Trafficking

"Stay safe, be safe"

"SAVE OUR CHILDREN, let's choose life"

The end. Thank you.

Life, Liberty and Injustice Organization Listings:

(For support, volunteering, donation and awareness in your area, to add to what's important to your needs)

Name: _____

Address: _____

City, State, Zip: _____

_____

Phone#: _____

Website: _____

Additional Information: _____

_____

Name: _____

Address: _____

City, State, Zip: _____

_____

Phone#: _____

Website: _____

Additional Information: _____

_____

Name: _____

Address: _____

City, State, Zip: _____

_____

Phone#: _____

Website: _____

Additional Information: _____

_____

Name: _____

Address: _____

City, State, Zip: _____

_____

Phone#: _____

Website: _____

Additional Information: _____

_____

Life, Liberty and Injustice Document Sheets:

(Documentation on Information for an Incident Report)

Name(s): _____

_____

Time(s): _____

Location(s): _____

Additional Information: _____

_____

_____

_____

_____

_____

_____

_____

_____

_____

_____

_____

_____

_____

Name(s): _____

_____

Time(s): _____

Location(s): _____

Additional Information: _____

_____

_____

_____

_____

_____

_____

_____

_____

_____

_____

_____

_____

_____

Life, Liberty and Injustice Journal:

KHADIJAH TIYA MUHAMMAD

LIFE, LIBERTY, AND INJUSTICE

About the Author

Khadijah Tiya Muhammad was an innovative and active person, always seeing the best in a person and wanting to get an understanding about people, places, and things around her by being active in school sports and community activities, working with the Red Cross as one, and being involved in politics in some form or fashion.

At an early age, she traveled and studied abroad, and her eyes have always enjoyed a cultural lifestyle being around people, places, and things. Her family has always been a modern family, so she knows of no line of difference but the skin and language. Once she had an encounter in Europe of being around persons at the time, students or a student sometimes with no arms, having to use their legs and feet to do everything like eat, write, etc. on a daily basis, that became a situation of understanding. Anything else to her was just living among people.

Being around people from all walks of life has always been good energy and joyful, knowing we are basically the same, just having different journeys to learn from or get through the day as a person. But realistically, your life maybe out of control. It may not be how you want it to be. The way you live and the things that matter may cause you to see it a lot differently, so she wants to make a difference for those who may not have an understanding how life can show's you it's ugly face or you may be a part of the problems in our community taking away a person's liberty or bring injustice to others in an unlawful way.

In 1993, living in Charleston, West Virginia, she ran for NAACP president and won. This is where it all began for her, and the world was changing in another strange way. She was asked to be on shows like *The Jerry Springer Show*, *The Phil Donahue Show*, college and local shows. She was nominated for the Jefferson Award in West Virginia, ABC Station Network, for her service to the community. In Detroit, she is working with other organizations as an activist and organizer, along with others in the community. One was "Keep the Vote, No Takeover."

We all watch our lives become more connected by so many injustices, hate, and more mental crimes. We stop needing each other and listening to what is being said and done to others, until *now*.

Because people need people.

CPSIA information can be obtained
at www.ICGtesting.com
Printed in the USA
LVHW071507121219
639936LV00057B/1024/P